CAMBRIDGE
UNIVERSITY PRESS

T0268620

Biology

for Cambridge IGCSE™

PRACTICAL WORKBOOK

Matthew Broderick

CAMBRIDGE
UNIVERSITY PRESS & ASSESSMENT

Shaftesbury Road, Cambridge CB2 8EA, United Kingdom

One Liberty Plaza, 20th Floor, New York, NY 10006, USA

477 Williamstown Road, Port Melbourne, VIC 3207, Australia

314–321, 3rd Floor, Plot 3, Splendor Forum, Jasola District Centre, New Delhi – 110025, India

103 Penang Road, #05–06/07, Visioncrest Commercial, Singapore 238467

Cambridge University Press & Assessment is a department of the University of Cambridge.

We share the University's mission to contribute to society through the pursuit of education, learning and research at the highest international levels of excellence.

www.cambridge.org
Information on this title: www.cambridge.org/9781108947497

© Cambridge University Press & Assessment 2021

First published 2017
Second edition 2021

20 19 18 17 16 15 14 13 12 11 10 9 8 7

Printed in Poland by Opolgraf

A catalogue record for this publication is available from the British Library

ISBN 978-1-108-94749-7 Practical Workbook with Digital Access (2 Years)

Additional resources for this publication at www.cambridge.org/go

Illustrations by Eleanor Jones

DEDICATED TEACHER AWARDS

Teachers play an important part in shaping futures. Our Dedicated Teacher Awards recognise the hard work that teachers put in every day.

Thank you to everyone who nominated this year; we have been inspired and moved by all of your stories. Well done to all of our nominees for your dedication to learning and for inspiring the next generation of thinkers, leaders and innovators.

Congratulations to our incredible winner and finalists!

WINNER

Patricia Abril	Stanley Manaay	Tiffany Cavanagh	Helen Comerford	John Nicko Coyoca	Meera Rangarajan
New Cambridge School, Colombia	Salvacion National High School, Philippines	Trident College Solwezi, Zambia	Lumen Christi Catholic College, Australia	University of San Jose-Recoletos, Philippines	RBK International Academy, India

For more information about our dedicated teachers and their stories, go to
dedicatedteacher.cambridge.org

CAMBRIDGE
UNIVERSITY PRESS

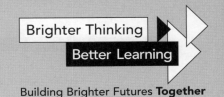

Brighter Thinking
Better Learning

Building Brighter Futures **Together**

> Contents

> How to use this series

We offer a comprehensive, flexible array of resources for the Cambridge IGCSE™ Biology syllabus. We provide targeted support and practice for the specific challenges we've heard that students face: learning science with English as a second language; learners who find the mathematical content within science difficult; and developing practical skills.

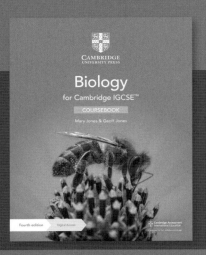

The coursebook provides coverage of the full Cambridge IGCSE Biology syllabus. Each chapter explains facts and concepts, and uses relevant real-world examples of scientific principles to bring the subject to life. Together with a focus on practical work and plenty of active learning opportunities, the coursebook prepares learners for all aspects of their scientific study. At the end of each chapter, examination-style questions offer practice opportunities for learners to apply their learning.

The digital teacher's resource contains detailed guidance for all topics of the syllabus, including common misconceptions identifying areas where learners might need extra support, as well as an engaging bank of lesson ideas for each syllabus topic. Differentiation is emphasised with advice for identification of different learner needs and suggestions of appropriate interventions to support and stretch learners. The teacher's resource also contains support for preparing and carrying out all the investigations in the practical workbook, including a set of sample results for when practicals aren't possible.

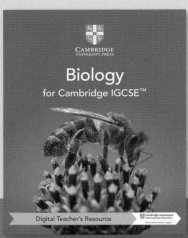

The teacher's resource also contains scaffolded worksheets and unit tests for each chapter. Answers for all components are accessible to teachers for free on the Cambridge GO platform.

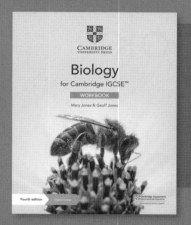

The skills-focused workbook has been carefully constructed to help learners develop the skills that they need as they progress through their Cambridge IGCSE Biology course, providing further practice of all the topics in the coursebook. A three-tier, scaffolded approach to skills development enables students to gradually progress through 'focus', 'practice' and 'challenge' exercises, ensuring that every learner is supported. The workbook enables independent learning and is ideal for use in class or as homework.

The practical workbook provides learners with additional opportunities for hands-on practical work, giving them full guidance and support that will help them to develop their investigative skills. These skills include planning investigations, selecting and handling apparatus, creating hypotheses, recording and displaying results, and analysing and evaluating data.

COMING IN 2022

Mathematics is an integral part of scientific study, and one that learners often find a barrier to progression in science. The Maths Skills for Cambridge IGCSE Biology write-in workbook has been written in collaboration with the Association of Science Education, with each chapter focusing on several maths skills that students need to succeed in their Biology course.

Our research shows that English language skills are the single biggest barrier to students accessing international science. This write-in English language skills workbook contains exercises set within the context of IGCSE Biology topics to consolidate understanding and embed practice in aspects of language central to the subject. Activities range from practising using 'effect' and 'affect' in the context of enzymes, to writing about expiration with a focus on common prefixes.

COMING IN 2022

> How to use this book

Throughout this book, you will notice lots of different features that will help your learning. These are explained below. Answers are accessible to teachers for free on the 'supporting resources' area of the Cambridge GO website.

INTRODUCTION

These set the scene for each chapter and indicate the important concepts. These start with the sentence 'The investigations in this chapter will:'.

KEY WORDS

Key vocabulary and definitions are given at the start of each investigation. You will also find definitions of these words in the Glossary at the back of this book.

COMMAND WORDS

Command words that appear in the syllabus and might be used in exams are highlighted in the exam-style questions. In the margin, you will find the Cambridge International definition. You will also find these definitions in the Glossary at the back of the book with some further explanation on the meaning of these words.

LEARNING INTENTIONS

These set out the learning intentions for each investigation.

The investigations include information on **equipment**, **safety considerations** and **method**. They also include **questions** to test your understanding on recording data, handling data, analysis and evaluation.

Remember that there is a **safety section** at the start of this book – you should refer to this often, as it contains general advice that is applicable to many of the investigations.

REFLECTION

These encourage you to reflect on your learning approaches.

> TIPS
>
> The information in these boxes will help you complete the questions, and give you support in areas that you might find difficult.

Supplement content

Where content is intended for students who are studying the Supplement content of the syllabus as well as the Core, this is indicated using the arrow and the bar, as on the left here.

> EXAM-STYLE QUESTIONS
>
> Questions at the end of each chapter provide more demanding exam-style questions, some of which may require use of knowledge from previous chapters. The answers to these questions are accessible to teachers for free on the Cambridge GO site.

Note for teachers:

The Teacher's Resource in this series includes sample data and support notes for each of the practical investigations in this practical workbook. You can find information about planning and setting up each investigation, further safety guidance, common errors to be aware of, differentiation ideas and additional areas for discussion.

Answers to all questions in this practical workbook are also accessible to teachers at www.cambridge.org/go

> Introduction

Many of the great biological discoveries of our time have been made as a result of scientific investigation. From the first recorded dissection in 1275, to the first compound microscope in the 16th century, to the work of Pasteur, Pavlov, Mendel, and Watson and Crick, practical biology has allowed the greatest scientific minds to measure and record their observations. These scientists followed the same scientific principles that you will follow in order to make their discoveries. It often took them years, and sometimes decades, to present their findings but do not worry, you will not have to do the same unless you are fortunate enough to work in practical biology for your career. The applications of practical biology cover much of science and could lead to careers in bioengineering, medicine, cancer research, plants and so much more. One important thing to remember is that sometimes discoveries can be serendipitous (discovered by accident, such as Tim Hunt's work on cyclins) so observe keenly and you may find out something that you were not even looking for.

Practical skills form the backbone of any biology course. It is hoped that, by using this book, you will gain confidence in this exciting and essential area of study. These interesting and enjoyable investigations are intended to kindle a passion for practical biology. This book has been written to prepare Cambridge IGCSE™ Biology students for their practical examinations and alternatives to examinations for Cambridge IGCSE Biology (0610/0970). It covers many of the investigation-focussed learning objectives. For either paper, you need to be able to demonstrate a wide range of practical skills. Through the various investigations and accompanying questions, you can build and refine your abilities so that you gain enthusiasm in tackling laboratory work. Great care has been taken to ensure that this book contains work that is safe and accessible for you to complete. Before attempting any of these activities, though, make sure that you have read the safety section and are following the safety regulations of the place where you study.

Answers to the exercises in this practical workbook can be found in the Teacher's Resource. Ask your teacher to provide access to the answers.

> Safety

Despite Bunsen burners and chemicals being used on a regular basis, the science laboratory is often one of the safest classrooms in a school. This is due to the emphasis on safety and the following of precautions set out by regular risk assessment and procedures.

It is important that you follow the safety rules set out by your teacher. Your teacher will know the names of materials and the hazards associated with them as part of their risk assessment for performing the investigations. They will share this information with you as part of their safety brief or demonstration of the investigation.

The safety precautions in each of the investigations of this book are guidance that you should follow. You should aim to use the safety rules as further direction to help to prepare for examination when planning your own investigations.

The following precautions will help to ensure your safety when carrying out most investigations in this workbook.

- Wear safety spectacles to protect your eyes.

- Tie back hair and any loose items of clothing.

- Personal belongings should be tidied away to avoid tripping over them.

- Wear gloves and protective clothing as described in the book or by your teacher.

- Turn the Bunsen burner to the yellow flame when not in use.

- Observe hazard symbols and chemical information provided with all substances and solutions.

Many of the investigations require some sort of teamwork or group work. It is the responsibility of your group to make sure that you plan how to be safe as diligently as you plan the rest of the investigation.

> Practical skills and support

The 'Experimental skills and investigations' outlined in the Cambridge IGCSE Biology syllabus focus on skills and abilities you need to develop to work as a scientist. Each of these aspects have been broken down for you below with a reference to the chapters in this title that cover it. This will enable you to identify where you have practised each skill and also allow you to revise each one before your exam.

Skills grid

Chapter	1	2	3	4	5	6	7	8	9	10	11	12	13	14	15	16	17	18	19	20
Experimental skills and investigations																				
1.1 demonstrate knowledge of how to safely use techniques																				
1.2 demonstrate knowledge of how to select and use apparatus and materials																				
1.3 demonstrate knowledge of how to follow a sequence of instructions																				
2 plan experiments and investigations																				
3.1 make and record observations																				
3.2 make and record measurements																				
3.3 make and record estimates																				
4.1 interpret experimental observations and data																				
4.2 evaluate experimental observations and data																				
5.1 evaluate methods																				
5.2 suggest possible improvements to methods																				
Additional Key Skills for Biology																				
Biological drawings or sketches																				
Constructing own table																				
Drawing/analysing a graph																				
Planning safety of an investigation																				
Mathematical calculations																				

Apparatus

You will need to be able to identify, use and draw a variety of scientific apparatus.

Complete the table below by adding a diagram and uses for each piece of apparatus.

Apparatus	Diagram	Uses
timer		
balance/scales		
beaker		
Pasteur/dropping pipette		

Apparatus	Diagram	Uses
conical flask		
Bunsen burner		
tripod		
test-tube / boiling tube		

Measuring

Being able to take accurate measurements is an essential skill for all biology students. As part of your course, you will be expected to be able to take accurate measurements using a variety of different apparatus. When using measuring cylinders, you will need to look for the meniscus, which is the bottom of the curve formed by the liquid.

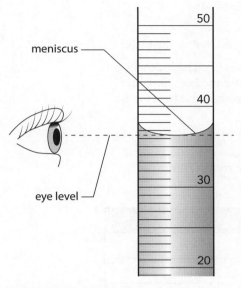

Thermometers are a very common tool for measuring temperature in biology experiments, so you will need to be able to take reliable readings. Not all of the points on the scale on a thermometer will be marked, but you will still need to be able to determine the temperature. To do this you will need to work out the value of each graduation. In the diagram on the right there are four marks between 95 and 100. Each of these marks indicates 1 °C.

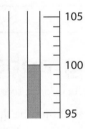

Biological drawings

It is important that you can draw what you see when observing biological specimens, whether it is under a microscope or you are using a magnifying glass, or you are observing with your eyes only. You are not expected to be an accomplished artist but your drawing should convey what you see as clearly as possible. Your drawings, sketches and diagrams should meet the following expectations:

- Drawn using a sharp pencil.

- Draw clear, unbroken lines.

- Do not use shading or colour.

- Drawn to scale unless stated otherwise.

- Drawn as large, or larger, than the specimen unless stated otherwise.

- Major structures or features should be clearly labelled using a ruler.

Recording

When working on investigations, the ability to record data accurately is very important. Sometimes a table will be supplied; however, you need to be able to draw your own table with the correct headings and units. The first task is to identify the independent and dependent variables for the investigation you are doing.

- The independent variable is the one that you are changing to see if this affects the dependent variable.

- The dependent variable is the one that you will measure and record the results of in the table.

The variables and their units need to go into the top two boxes in your results table. The independent variable goes in the left-hand box and the dependent variable goes in the right-hand box. Separate the name of the variables and units using a forward slash /, e.g. time / s. Remember that the column headings need to be physical quantities (time, mass, temperature, etc.)

Next, count how many different values you have for the independent variable. This is how many rows you will need to add below the column headings. Finally, add the values for the independent variable into the left-hand column. Your table is now ready for you to add the results from your investigation in the right-hand column.

Independent variable / units	Dependent variable / units

Drawing graphs

The type of graph you choose to draw is likely to depend on the type of data you are recording:

- Pie charts: These should be drawn with the sectors in rank order, largest first, beginning at 'noon' and proceeding clockwise. Pie charts should preferably contain no more than six sectors.

- Bar charts: These should be drawn when one of the variables is not numerical. They should be made up of narrow blocks of equal width that do not touch.

- Histograms: These should be drawn when plotting frequency graphs with continuous data. The blocks should be drawn in order of increasing or decreasing magnitude and they should touch.

Whichever type of graph you draw, however, it is useful to follow a set procedure every time to ensure that, when you are finished, the graph is complete.

Axes – You must label the axes with your independent and dependent variables. The independent variable is used to label the x-axis (horizontal axis) and the dependent variable is used to label the y-axis (vertical axis). Remember to also add the units for each of the variables. An easy way to ensure that you get this correct is to copy the column headings from the table of data you are using to draw the graph.

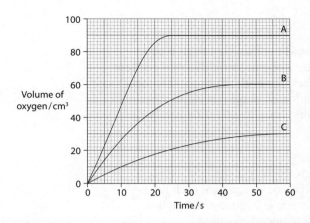

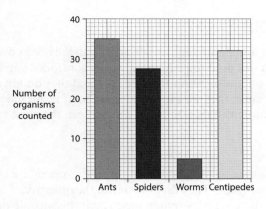

TIP

At the top of any table of data you have to use, write the letters X and Y next to the independent and dependent variable to remind you which axis each goes on.

The second stage of drawing a graph is adding a scale. You must select a scale that allows you to use more than half of the graph grid in both directions. Choose a sensible ratio to allow you to easily plot your points (e.g. each 1 cm on the graph grid represents 1, 2, 5, 10, 50 or 100 units of the variable). If you choose to use other numbers for your scale, it becomes much more difficult to plot your graph. This skill gets easier the more times you draw a graph. If you have done this lightly with a pencil, you can easily make adjustments until you are fully skilled.

Now you are ready to plot the points of data on the graph grid. You can use either crosses (×) or a point enclosed inside a circle to plot your points but take your time to make sure these are plotted accurately. Remember to use a sharp pencil as large dots make it difficult to see the place the point is plotted and may make it difficult for the accuracy of the plot to be decided.

Finally, a best-fit line needs to be added. This must be a single thin line or smooth curve. It does not need to go through all of the points but it should have roughly half the number of points on each side of the data scattered. Remember to ignore any anomalous data when you draw your best-fit line. Some good examples of best-fit lines are shown below:

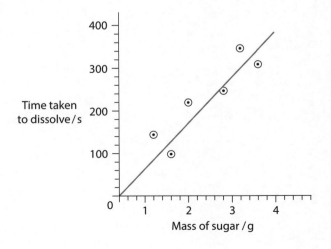

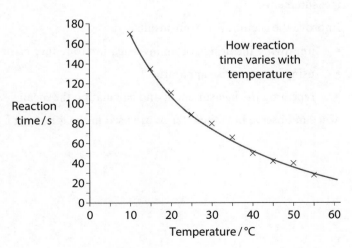

Variables

The independent and dependent variables have already been discussed but there is a third type of variable that you will need to be familiar with – controlled variables. These are variables that are kept the same during an investigation to make sure that they do not affect the results. If these variables are not kept the same, then we cannot be sure that it is our independent variable having an effect on the results. The more variables that you can control, the more reliable your investigation will be.

Example

Two students are investigating how changing the temperature affects the rate at which starch is broken down by amylase. They do not control the quantity of amylase or starch used each time. This means that there is no pattern in their results because, if they use more starch and amylase, the amount of glucose produced will be increased regardless of the temperatures used.

Reliability, accuracy and precision

A common task in this book will be to suggest how to improve the method used in an investigation to improve its reliability/accuracy/precision. Before we come to how these improvements can be made, it is important that you have an understanding of what each of these words means.

Reliability is about the likelihood of getting the same results if you did the investigation again and being sure that the results are not just down to chance. Reliability is now often called repeatability for this reason. If you can repeat an investigation several times and get the same result each time, it is said to be reliable.

Improve the reliability of your investigation by:

- repeating the experiment until no anomalous results are achieved.

Precise results have very little deviance from the mean.

Improve the precision of your investigation by:

- using apparatus that has smaller scale divisions.

Accuracy is a measure of how close the measured value is to the true value. The accuracy of the results depends on the measuring apparatus used and the skill of the person taking the measurements.

Improve the accuracy of your results by:

- improving the design of an investigation to reduce errors

- using more precise apparatus

- repeating the measurement and calculating the mean.

You can observe how these terms are used in the following figure.

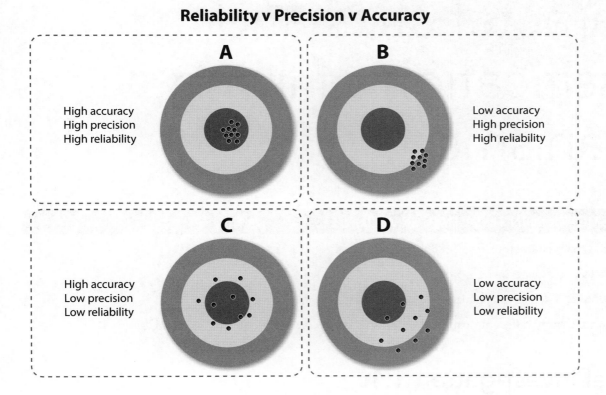

Reliability v Precision v Accuracy

A — High accuracy, High precision, High reliability

B — Low accuracy, High precision, High reliability

C — High accuracy, Low precision, Low reliability

D — Low accuracy, Low precision, Low reliability

Validity

Validity is the confidence that scientists put into a set of results and the conclusions that they draw from them. Results are considered valid if they measure what they were designed to, and if they are precise, accurate and reliable.

Designing an investigation

When asked to design an investigation, you must think carefully about what level of detail to include. The following is an example of how to create a method. Follow these steps to be able to design reliable, accurate investigations.

1 Identify what your independent variable is and the range of values that you are planning to use for it.

2 The dependent variable must also be identified along with how (using equipment and apparatus) you are going to measure it.

3 Suggest how you will control other variables.

4 Outline the method in a series of numbered steps that is detailed enough for someone else to follow.

5 Remember to include repeat readings to help improve reliability.

6 Check the validity of your investigation and results.

7 You must also include any hazards and safety warnings, as well as safety equipment that should be used in the investigation.

Characteristics and classification of living organisms

THE INVESTIGATION IN THIS CHAPTER WILL:

- review the main characteristics of different organisms
- help you to construct a dichotomous key
- enable you to practise your biological drawing skills
- help you to identify different groups of organisms based on the organisms' external features.

Practical investigation 1.1: Construct a dichotomous key

KEY WORDS

biological drawing: used to represent the visible features of an organism, in the correct size, shape and proportion

dichotomous key: a way of identifying an organism, by working through pairs of statements that lead you to its name

feature: parts of an organism that you can see; also known as characteristics, e.g. the fur of a mammal

magnification: how many times larger an image is than the actual object. If an object is drawn smaller than its actual size, then the magnification is less than 1.

IN THIS INVESTIGATION YOU WILL:

- construct a dichotomous key that is relevant to your local area
- make a biological drawing and use the drawing to identify an organism.

Safety

- Ensure that the leaves are free from other organisms.

- Wash your hands after handling any organisms.

- Think about the safety requirements for *your* chosen environment. What do you need to look out for, or be aware of?

Getting started

Think about the main features of the organisms that you are looking at. What should you be looking for? For example, when you are looking for suitable specimens, you might choose to consider the different structure of leaves.

Method

1   If you are collecting organisms yourself, gather the equipment required (if you are collecting invertebrates then you may require equipment such as a pooter). Otherwise, use the organisms provided for you by your teacher.

2   Search for, and collect, at least three organisms that have different features. Use the equipment provided that is most suitable for organisms that you intend to collect.

3   Return to the laboratory or classroom with your organisms. Identify the different features that might help you to put the organisms into different groups.

4 Draw a draft dichotomous key in the space below. You should begin by looking for features that might distinguish one organism from another. Try to keep your answers simple, using 'yes' and 'no'. Sometimes, this takes a bit of trial and error so use a pencil at first and do not be afraid to change your questions or answers at any point.

> **TIP**
>
> When constructing a dichotomous key, use the most obvious features that you can actually *see*.

5 When you have completed your key, work with a partner to test the key with your chosen organisms.

6 Once you are happy that your key works, you can construct your final dichotomous key and ask other people in the class to use it.

Recording data

1   Make a large drawing of one of your organisms in the space below. Label the drawing.

2   State the features of your organism that help you to identify which group the organism belongs to.

....

....

3   State the group that your organism belongs to.

....

Handling data

4   Use a ruler to measure the length of the actual organism. Then use the ruler to measure the length of your drawing of that organism. Use this information to calculate the magnification of your drawing.

....

....

....

> **TIP**
>
> Try to use millimetres as your unit of measurement as millimetres are much easier to convert into other units if required.
>
> Remember, the magnification is the image size, divided by the actual size.

> **TIP**
>
> When you are finished, organisms should be returned back to their habitat to ensure they are not harmed and to limit the impact of the investigation.

Analysis

5 Analyse your drawing skills. How many of the skills below have you used when drawing your specimen? Tick the ones that you have used correctly. These are important skills when making a biological drawing.

Drawing skills	I have done this
I used a sharp pencil.	
I drew smooth, single lines.	
I drew the specimen in the correct shape and proportion.	
The drawing is larger than the actual specimen (where possible).	
I have drawn all observable features.	
I used a ruler to draw neat lines from the labels to the drawing. Each line touches the feature that the line identifies.	
I have not shaded the diagram, or used colours.	

Evaluation

6 Suggest why it is important you follow the 'rules' when making a biological drawing.

....

....

> **REFLECTION**
>
> Using the checklist above, how could you improve your biological drawings?
>
> ....
>
> ....

1   The adult housefly (*Musca domestica*) is found in many countries around
the world.

a   Make a larger drawing of the adult housefly in the space provided.   [5]

b   Measure the actual size of the length of one of the wings in the figure.

.... [1]

c   **Calculate** the magnification of the same wing on your drawing of
the figure. Give your answer to three significant figures.

....

....

.... [2]

d   **State** the binomial name of the adult housefly.

.... [1]

e   **Identify** the features of the housefly that would place it in the insect group.

....

.... [2]

[Total: 11]

COMMAND WORDS

calculate: work out
from given facts,
figures or information

state: express in
clear terms

identify: name/
select/recognise

Chapter 2

Cells

THE INVESTIGATIONS IN THIS CHAPTER WILL:

- help you to prepare a specimen of a plant cell and an animal cell
- allow you to observe specimens of plant cells and animal cells under the microscope
- help you to identify key features of some specialised cells.

Practical investigation 2.1: Observing plant cells

KEY WORDS

light microscope: a type of microscope that uses light and a lens to magnify a specimen

magnification: how many times larger an image is than the actual object. If an object is drawn smaller than its actual size, then the magnification is less than 1.

specimen: a prepared slide that contains something to be viewed under a microscope

staining solution: used to make cells more visible on a microscope slide, such as iodine or methylene blue

IN THIS INVESTIGATION YOU WILL:

- develop your microscope skills using a light microscope
- observe key features of plant cells and link them to the cells' functions.

YOU WILL NEED:

- light microscope • microscope slides • coverslips
- forceps • scalpel • mounted needle • safety spectacles
- staining solution, such 1% methylene blue, or iodine • 1 whole onion • paper towel.

Safety

- Report broken slides or coverslips to your teacher.
- Do not touch the microscope lens as it may become very hot.
- Store scalpels safely when not in use.

Getting started

Use a prepared microscope slide to familiarise yourself with how the microscope works. Begin with looking at a low magnification before increasing the magnification. Can you recall which parts help you to focus what you see?

Method

1 Set up the microscope as demonstrated by your teacher.

2 Remove a single layer of onion using a scalpel or forceps. This may be tricky to do at first but by removing the top layer of the onion, you should find that a thin layer will start to present itself.

3 Place the layer of cells onto the microscope slide, ensuring that there are as few folds or creases as possible.

4 Add a drop of your staining solution to the onion. The smaller the drop of solution the better, as this will avoid 'flooding' the slide.

> **TIP**
>
> When placing the drop of staining solution onto the onion cells, try to lower the drop from the pipette onto the onion. This will help you to get the smallest amount of solution onto the specimen and will help you see your cells clearly.

5 Use a paper towel to absorb any excess solution.

6 Lower the coverslip onto the sample at an angle of 45 degrees, as shown in Figure 2.1. The coverslip should fall gently onto the sample.

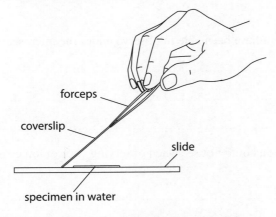

Figure 2.1: Technique required to lower the coverslip onto the slide.

7 Using the end of a pencil, tap the coverslip lightly to press it down onto the sample of onion.

8 Place the prepared slide onto the microscope stage.

9 Turn on the microscope and starting at the lowest magnification of your microscope, turn the focusing wheel until you can see your specimen.

10 Use the fine focusing wheel to make the image sharper.

Recording data

1 Using the circles below, draw what you can see through two of the magnifications that you use. At the lowest magnification, you may view hundreds of cells, so it might be more suitable to only draw a few cells.

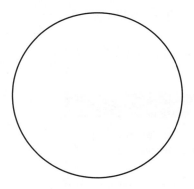
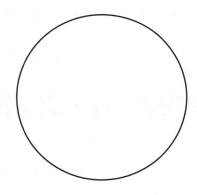

Magnification: ....   Magnification: ....

2 Label the key features that you can see in your observed cells.

Analysis

3 State the function of the features that you have been able to observe under the microscope.

....

....

....

4 State the structures of a plant cell that you could not see when observing your onion cells under the microscope.

....

5 Explain why you could not see the structures named in Question **4**.

....

Evaluation

6 Explain why it was important you used a single layer of onion cells for this investigation.

....

....

7 Suggest what you would see under the microscope if you did not use a staining solution.

....

....

Practical investigation 2.2: Observing animal cells

IN THIS INVESTIGATION YOU WILL:

- develop your microscope skills using a light microscope
- observe key features of animal cells and link them to the cells' functions.

YOU WILL NEED:

- light microscope • cotton buds • disinfectant solution
- staining solution (such as iodine or 1% methylene blue) • microscope slides
- coverslips • mounting needle • safety spectacles • paper towel.

Safety

- Cotton buds must be placed into the disinfectant solution immediately after use.
- Report any broken microscope slides or coverslips to your teacher immediately.
- Do not touch the microscope lens as it may become very hot.

Getting started

What do you think you will see when you observe animal cells in the investigation? Compare this to what you saw in the plant cells. What are the differences you expect to observe?

Method

1   Set up the microscope safely as you have done so previously.

2   Using a cotton bud, scrape the inside of your cheek. This should be done with some pressure while rotating the bud to ensure that you collect the maximum cheek cells possible.

3   Using the same rotating action, apply the cotton bud to your microscope slide. You should do this in the centre of the slide so that you know exactly where your cells should be.

4   Using the same technique that you used in Investigation 2.1, add part of a drop of the staining solution to the area on the slide where you placed your cheek cells.

5   Use a paper towel to absorb any excess solution.

6   Lower the coverslip at an angle of 45 degrees.

7   Using the end of a pencil, tap the coverslip lightly to press it down onto the sample.

8   Place the prepared slide onto the microscope stage.

9   Turn on the microscope and starting at the lowest magnification of your microscope, turn the focusing wheel until you can see your specimen.

10 Use the fine focusing wheel to make the image sharper.

Recording data

1   Using the circles below, draw what you can see at each magnification. At the lowest magnification, you may view many cells, so it might be more suitable to only draw a few cells.

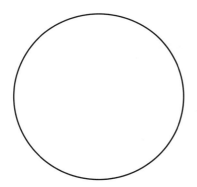

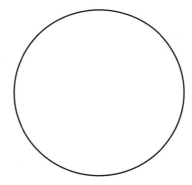

Magnification: ....

Magnification: ....

Analysis

2 Identify the key features of your cheek cells that you could see through the light microscope.

....

3 State the function of the features that you identified in Question **2**.

....

....

....

4 It was not possible to see any mitochondria using your light microscope. State the function of the mitochondria.

....

Evaluation

5 Explain why the cotton buds were placed into disinfectant or sterilising solution after being used to collect the cell sample.

....

REFLECTION

How could you improve this investigation so that you could see all of the different structures of an animal cell under a light microscope?

....

....

....

Practical investigation 2.3: Drawing biological specimens

IN THIS INVESTIGATION YOU WILL:

- observe specialised cells and tissues under the microscope

- practise your biological drawing skills.

YOU WILL NEED:

- light microscope   • prepared slides of different cells and tissues.

Safety

- Report any broken microscope slides or coverslips to your teacher immediately.

- Do not touch the microscope lens as this may become very hot.

Getting started

Look at the slides that you have been given. Discuss with a partner what you might expect to see when observed under the microscope. What do you think are the key features of each cell / tissue that you will observe?

Method

1   Set up your microscope.

2   View the different slides available under your microscope, using the different magnifications to obtain a clear view of each specimen.

Recording data

1 Make labelled drawings of what you see in the spaces below. Include a description of what you were looking at and the magnification of the microscope.

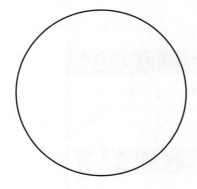
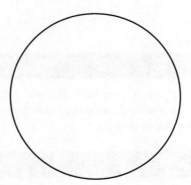

Magnification: ....

Specimen: ....

Magnification: ....

Specimen: ....

> **TIP**
> You should ensure that you are meeting all of the criteria of a good biological drawing.

Handling data

2 Calculate the total magnification for each of your drawings and write this next to your drawings.

Analysis

3 For each of your specimens, explain how their specialised features allow each specimen to carry out their function.

....

....

....

....

....

Evaluation

4   Explain why it is important that the drawings are labelled.

....

....

REFLECTION

Exchange your drawings with a partner and use the table below to assess the quality of their biological drawings. Ask the person who is assessing your work to write comments about how to improve your drawings.

Drawing skills	I have done this (peer assessment)
A sharp pencil has been used.	
Smooth, single lines have been drawn.	
Drawn the specimen in the correct shape and proportion.	
The drawing is larger than the actual specimen (where possible).	
All observable features have been drawn.	
Labelled lines are drawn neatly with a ruler and touching the feature that they identify.	
No shading or colours have been used.	

EXAM-STYLE QUESTIONS

1 Look at the leaf shown in the figure.

a Make a large, detailed drawing of this leaf. [5]

b Measure the length of the leaf in the figure.

.... [1]

c Measure the length of your drawing of the leaf.

.... [1]

d **Calculate** the magnification of your drawing.

....

....

.... [3]

[Total: 10]

COMMAND WORD

calculate: work out from given facts, figures or information

> Chapter 3

Movement into and out of cells

THE INVESTIGATIONS IN THIS CHAPTER WILL:

- show how diffusion and osmosis occur in real-life examples

- encourage you to make predictions about how substances move into and out of cells.

Practical investigation 3.1: Diffusion with sweets

KEY WORD

diffusion: the net movement of particles from a region of their higher concentration to a region of their lower concentration (i.e. down a concentration gradient), as a result of their random movement

IN THIS INVESTIGATION YOU WILL:

- observe how diffusion occurs in a liquid

- suggest ideas for altering the rate of diffusion.

YOU WILL NEED:

- large Petri dish (or other similar white / clear plate or dish)   • water
- sweets that are coated with coloured sugar shells.

Safety

Do not eat the sweets.

Getting started

Before you do this investigation, what do you think will happen to the colour of the sweets when placed into water? What do you think the colour of the water will be?

Method

1   Place the sweets around the inner perimeter of the Petri dish, alternating the colours as much as possible, as shown in Figure 3.1.

Figure 3.1: Arrangement of sweets in the Petri dish.

2   Carefully add water to the inside of the Petri dish. Do this by pouring the water into the centre of the dish until the sweets are submerged halfway. Pour slowly so that the sweets are not dislodged from their starting position.

> **TIP**
>
> If the sweets move away from the edge of the dish when the water is poured, simply move them quickly and carefully back to their original position.

3   Observe what happens to the colouring of the sweets and the water.

Recording data

1   Record the time it takes for the colours to reach the middle of the dish.

....

2   Make a sketch of what happens to your sweets and water.

Analysis

3   Explain why the colour of the sweets moved towards the centre of the dish.

....

Evaluation

4   Suggest and explain what would happen if you used warm water for this investigation.

....

5   Design a method to show how you could measure the effect that a range of different water
temperatures would have for the same investigation.

....

....

....

....

....

....

6   Suggest what would happen if you replaced water with hydrochloric acid for this investigation.

....

....

REFLECTION

Did you achieve the expected pattern? If not, how could you improve the technique of
adding the water?

....

....

Practical investigation 3.2: Diffusion in gelatine

KEY WORDS

concentration gradient: an imaginary 'slope' from a high concentration to a low concentration

IN THIS INVESTIGATION YOU WILL:

- observe diffusion in action using gelatine
- explain what you observe using your knowledge of diffusion.

YOU WILL NEED:

- red gelatine or jelly   • scalpel   • 1 mol dm⁻³ hydrochloric acid   • test-tube and bung.

Safety

- Take care when using the scalpel.
- Wear safety spectacles at all times.
- Take care when using the acid.

Getting started

With a partner, make predictions about what will happen to a piece of gelatine / jelly when placed in a test-tube full of hydrochloric acid. Consider how the surface area to volume ratio might influence the results.

Method

1   Cut a piece of gelatine to fit inside your test-tube (1 cm × 1 cm × 1 cm).

2   Place in the test-tube and add enough hydrochloric acid to cover the gelatine.

3   Place the bung firmly into the top of the test-tube.

4   Place the test-tube horizontally, using two solid objects either side to ensure that the test-tube does not roll off the table.

5   Observe what happens to the colour of the gelatine.

Recording data

1   Write down what happened to the colour of the gelatine and record the time taken for all of the colour to be gone.

....

Analysis

2   Using your knowledge of diffusion, explain what caused the observations that you made. You should aim to use the key words *concentration gradient* in your answer.

....

....

....

Evaluation

3   You used 1 mol dm^{-3} hydrochloric acid for this investigation. How could you make this reaction happen faster?

....

....

4   While repeating the experiment with different concentrations of acid, what steps would you take to ensure that your investigation is reliable?

....

....

....

Practical investigation 3.3: Osmosis in beetroot

KEY WORD

osmosis: the diffusion of water molecules through a partially permeable membrane

IN THIS INVESTIGATION YOU WILL:

- gather reliable data to support your knowledge of osmosis

- carry out a real-life application of osmosis.

YOU WILL NEED:

- beetroot   • cork borer   • clear, plastic ruler   • distilled water
- 30% sucrose solution   • 60% sucrose solution   • test-tube × 6   • test-tube rack
- scalpel   • whiteboard pen for writing on test-tubes   • safety spectacles.

Safety

Take care when using the cork borer and scalpel.

Getting started

Can you recall the definition for osmosis? In the space below, sketch a diagram to show your understanding of what happens to the water molecules during osmosis. You will need to visualise these when interpreting your results.

Method

1 Use the cork borer to bore out six pieces of beetroot of similar length.

2 Use the ruler and scalpel to cut the beetroot pieces to exactly the same length.

3 Record this length in the table in the Recording data section, below.

4 Pour the same amount of distilled water into two of the test-tubes and mark them 'A' for identification.

5 Pour the same amount of 30% sucrose solution into two of the test-tubes and mark them 'B' for identification.

6 Pour the same amount of 60% sucrose solution into two of the test-tubes and mark them 'C' for identification.

7 Add the beetroot to the test-tubes at the same time.

8 After 15 minutes, remove the beetroot from solution and pat dry using a paper towel.

9 Measure the length of each piece of beetroot and record in the table.

Recording data

1 Use the table below to record your results. Add the units to your table headings.

Solution	Length before			Length after			Average change in length
	beetroot 1	beetroot 2	average	beetroot 1	beetroot 2	average	
Water							
30% sucrose							
60% sucrose							

Handling data

2 Describe the method used to calculate the average change in the length of beetroot.

....

....

3 Calculate the percentage change of the beetroot before and after the investigation.

....

....

....

Analysis

4   Explain your results. Which solutions caused the beetroot to change size and why?

....

....

....

....

Evaluation

5   Measuring the change in length is not the most reliable method of observing the movement due to osmosis. Design a method for how you could measure the change in size of the beetroot with greater accuracy.

....

....

....

....

....

....

REFLECTION

Were you able to put all of the pieces of beetroot into the test-tubes at the same time? How might this have affected your results?

....

....

Practical investigation 3.4: Osmotic turgor

KEY WORDS

osmotic turgor: the force within a cell when the water pressure is applied against the walls of the cell

IN THIS INVESTIGATION YOU WILL:

- investigate osmotic turgor using dialysis tubing

- apply your knowledge of diffusion and osmosis to explain what happens in the dialysis tubing.

YOU WILL NEED:

- test-tube and rack • sugar solution • 20 cm dialysis tubing • distilled water
- elastic band • graduated pipette • safety spectacles.

Getting started

Remind yourself of the definitions of diffusion and osmosis. Look at the list of materials for this investigation and consider what sort of molecules might move from one place to another. Write your predictions below for comparison to the real results.

Method

1 Tie a tight knot in one end of the dialysis tubing.

2 Now, carefully open the opposite end of the dialysis tubing.

TIP

Once you have opened one end of the dialysis tubing slightly, you can insert a pipette to blow the rest of the tubing open. This is much easier than trying to prise the tubing open fully with your fingers.

3 Using the graduated pipette, add 4 cm³ of the sugar solution to the other end of the tubing and tightly knot that end.

4   Wash the outside of the tubing in cold water.

5   Place the tubing inside the test-tube (you can secure this by using an elastic band to secure the excess tubing after the knot).

6   Fill the test-tube with distilled water and leave for 30 minutes.

Recording data

1   Sketch a diagram to show the initial experimental setup, and a diagram to show what happened to the water and the tubing after the investigation.

before	after

Analysis

2   Describe the difference between the tube before the investigation and after the investigation.

....

....

3   Explain the changes that occurred during the investigation.

....

....

....

Evaluation

4   Suggest how you could change this method to make the movement of water happen faster.

....

....

....

EXAM-STYLE QUESTIONS

1 A student carried out an investigation to observe osmosis in potatoes. She recorded her results as shown in the table.

Solution	Mass of potato / g		
	Before	After	Change
Distilled water	1.30	1.79	
	1.31	1.71	
	1.21	1.66	
20% sucrose solution	1.51	1.45	
	1.60	1.53	
	1.69	1.43	
40% sucrose solution	1.40		
	1.40		
	1.40		

a **Calculate** the change in mass for each sample of potato.

....

....

.... [2]

b Calculate the average change in mass of the potatoes placed in distilled water and those placed in the 20% sucrose solution.

....

....

.... [3]

c **Describe** and **explain** the changes that occurred to the potato in the investigation.

....

....

.... [4]

d In the table, **predict** what the mass of potato might be after being placed into a 40% sucrose solution. Write your answers in the table and complete the 'change' column. [2]

[Total: 11]

COMMAND WORDS

calculate: work out from given facts, figures or information

describe: state the points of a topic / give characteristics and main features

explain: set out purposes or reasons / make the relationships between things evident / provide why and/or how and support with relevant evidence

predict: suggest what may happen based on available information

> Chapter 4
Biological molecules

THE INVESTIGATIONS IN THIS CHAPTER WILL:

- support your understanding of how to test for vitamin C

- plan and select the appropriate method for testing foodstuffs

- help you to extract your own DNA and relate your observations to your knowledge of the structure of DNA.

Practical investigation 4.1: Vitamin C in oranges

KEY WORD

DCPIP: a purple liquid that becomes colourless when mixed with vitamin C

IN THIS INVESTIGATION YOU WILL:

- test for the presence of vitamin C

- compare the difference in vitamin C between different oranges.

YOU WILL NEED:

- DCPIP solution • pipettes • test-tubes
- different sources of vitamin C (in this case it is oranges from different parts of the world, such as the Middle East, India, Spain, etc.)
- mass balance • measuring cylinders • safety spectacles.

Safety

DCPIP is harmful if ingested and should not be poured into sinks or drains.

Getting started

This investigation requires you to observe a colour change by slowly adding orange juice to a solution using a pipette. Before doing the investigation, practise using the pipette by using water and a beaker until you are able to successfully add single drops at a time.

> **TIP**
>
> When dropping solution from a pipette, apply as little pressure as you can with your fingers. You may also use your 'free' hand to balance / steady your dropping hand.

Method

1   Your teacher will provide you with the appropriate number of oranges. These may be from different regions or countries.

2   Extract $25\,cm^3$ of juice from each orange by squeezing the juice (by hand) directly into a measuring cylinder, or by using the mass balance ($1\,cm^3 = 1\,g$).

3   Add $1\,cm^3$ of DCPIP into the bottom of a test-tube. Label the test-tube with the type of orange juice to be added.

4   Using a pipette, slowly add the orange juice from the first type of orange to the DCPIP and stop adding when the DCPIP has turned colourless.

5   Calculate the amount of orange juice needed to turn the DCPIP colourless (amount added (cm^3) = $25\,cm^3$ – amount left over (cm^3)). Add the results to your results table in the Recording data section below.

6   Repeat the method for each of the different type of orange that you are using.

Recording data

1   Construct a table that will allow you to record your findings. Your table should include the types of orange and the amount of juice required to turn the DCPIP colourless.

Analysis

2 Describe the results of your investigation.

....

....

....

....

....

> **TIP**
>
> When describing your results, you should be describing any patterns that you can see in the data. You should be aiming to state any trends or relationships that have presented themselves. You should also be able to make a statement about which oranges had the most (or the least) vitamin C.

Evaluation

3 You tested each type of orange once. Suggest what you would do to improve the reliability of your investigation.

....

....

....

4 What other types of oranges could be tested to compare vitamin C content?

....

....

....

....

....

5 How could you improve the accuracy of your results to ensure that human error is removed from the observing of the colour change?

....

....

....

> **REFLECTION**
>
> Do you think that everyone in your class would agree with exactly when the DCPIP turned colourless? If not, why not, and how might this affect your results?
>
> ....
>
> ....
>
> ....

Practical investigation 4.2: Testing foods

KEY WORDS

Benedict's solution: a blue liquid that turns orange-red when heated with reducing sugar

biuret reagent: a blue solution that turns purple when mixed with amino acids or proteins

fat: lipids that are solid at room temperature

iodine solution: a solution of iodine in potassium iodide; it is orange-brown, and turns blue-black when mixed with starch

protein: a substance whose molecules are made of many amino acids linked together; each different protein has a different sequence of amino acids

reducing sugars: sugars such as glucose, which turn Benedict's solution orange-red when heated together

starch: a carbohydrate that is used as an energy store in plant cells

IN THIS INVESTIGATION YOU WILL:

- apply your knowledge to test different foodstuffs and find out what biological molecules they contain
- plan and select the appropriate method for testing foodstuffs.

YOU WILL NEED:

- test-tubes and/or spotting tiles • water • test-tube rack • alcohol
- pipettes • range of food and drink • pestle and mortar
- hot water (water-bath) • safety spectacles • biuret reagent
- iodine solution • ethanol solution • Benedict's solution.

Safety

Be careful with chemicals. Never ingest them and always wash your hands after handling them.

1 State two further safety requirements that you will need to follow for this investigation.

....

....

Method

2 Select three different types of food or drink substances from the selection available and outline a suitable test to determine if they contain reducing sugars, protein, starch or fat. In the following spaces, plan a method to carry out the tests.

Test 1

....

....

....

....

....

Test 2

....

....

....

....

....

Test 3

....

....

....

....

....

Recording data

3   Complete the table to show the results of your tests.

Food/drink	Test for reducing sugar	Test for protein	Test for fat	Test for starch

Analysis

4   For each of the foodstuffs that you tested, describe what you observed and state the biological molecules that each food contained.

....

....

....

....

....

> **TIP**
>
> It is important that you identify the colour change from X to Y. For example, the colour changed from blue to red. If there is no change, you should still state the colours that you see. For example, the colour remained blue, or there was no change from the colour blue.

Evaluation

5 How could your investigation be improved or the results be made more reliable?

....

....

REFLECTION

What did you find difficult about testing so many different foods? How could you improve on this problem?

....

....

Practical investigation 4.3: Extracting DNA

KEY WORD

DNA: a molecule that contains genetic information, in the form of genes, that controls the proteins that are made in the cell

IN THIS INVESTIGATION YOU WILL:

- follow an exact method to extract and observe your own DNA
- relate your observations to your knowledge of the structure of DNA.

YOU WILL NEED:

- drinking water • salt • clear drinking cups • food colouring
- washing-up liquid • glass beaker × 2 • glass rods
- $100 \, cm^3$ isopropyl alcohol solution • safety spectacles.

Safety

- Do not ingest the substances used in the investigation.
- Keep isopropyl alcohol away from naked flames.
- Wash your hands after the investigation.

Getting started

Successful application of the method in this investigation requires a steady hand when pouring the alcohol / food colouring mix (see Method step 8). Practise the technique with water and food colouring and see if you can do so slower than your partner.

Method

1   Mix 100 cm³ of drinking water with a tablespoon of salt in the beaker. Stir until all of the salt has dissolved.

2   Transfer approximately 50 cm³ of the saltwater into a drinking cup.

3   Gargle all of the water around your mouth for 60 seconds (take care not to swallow any of the water).

4   Spit the water back into a glass beaker.

5   Add a small drop of washing up liquid to the saltwater.

6   Use the glass rod to stir gently without causing any air bubbles.

7   Add three drops of food colouring to the isopropyl alcohol solution in a clean beaker.

8   Tilt the beaker to about 45 degrees and gently pour the alcohol / food colouring mix into the saltwater beaker. The alcohol mixture should trickle slowly down the side to reach the saltwater mix as slowly as possible.

9   The alcohol mixture will form a layer on top of the saltwater if you pour slowly enough.

10 Leave the solution for three minutes and observe the white clumps that form – this is your DNA.

> **TIP**
>
> When pouring the alcohol mixture into the beaker, try to be the slowest in the class; this way you will give yourself the best chance of achieving the separation of the DNA.

Recording data

1   In the space below, sketch a diagram of your DNA suspended in the solution. If you were not successful, you can observe the DNA of one of your peers.

Analysis

2   Describe the shape of the DNA in the suspension. Does this match your prior knowledge of the structure of DNA?

....

....

3   Suggest what the role of the washing up liquid was. This is a difficult question but the answer is linked to the location of the DNA within the cell.

....

....

Evaluation

4   Not everyone is able to achieve an extraction of DNA. Why do you think this is?

....

....

EXAM-STYLE QUESTIONS

1 A student carries out an investigation and tests three different types of food and records her results in the table below.

Food substance	Original colour	End colour
A	Blue	Purple
B	Blue	Blue
C	Blue	Purple

a **Identify** the substance that the student was most likely using to test these foods.

.... [1]

b **State** the nutrient that the student was testing for.

.... [1]

c State the positive result that you would expect for this food test.

.... [1]

d State which foods (A, B, C) produced a positive result for the student's investigation.

.... [1]

e **Explain** your answer to part **d**.

....

.... [2]

[Total: 6]

2 Many foods contain different amounts of reducing sugars. Plan a method that would allow you to test for the presence of reducing sugars. Your method must include the expected positive results for your test, as well as all safety considerations.

....

....

....

....

....

....

....

.... [8]

COMMAND WORDS

identify: name/ select/recognise

state: express in clear terms

explain: set out purposes or reasons / make the relationships between things evident / provide why and/or how and support with relevant evidence

Chapter 5

Enzymes

THE INVESTIGATIONS IN THIS CHAPTER WILL:

- show how enzymes work

- show the effect of temperature and hydrogen peroxide concentration on enzyme activity.

Practical investigation 5.1:
Effect of amylase on starch

KEY WORD

amylase: an enzyme that catalyses the breakdown of starch to maltose

IN THIS INVESTIGATION YOU WILL:

- observe how amylase affects starch, using the correct test to identify the products of the reaction

- apply your knowledge of food tests to your understanding of the structure of carbohydrates.

YOU WILL NEED:

- test-tube × 4 • 2% starch solution • Benedict's solution
- 5% amylase solution • test-tube rack • Bunsen burner • pipette × 3
- iodine solution • 250 cm³ glass beaker • safety spectacles • tripod
- gauze mat • heat mat • marker pen.

Safety

- Be careful with chemicals. Never ingest them and always wash your hands after handling them.

- Leave the water-bath to cool for several minutes after use.

- Use the Bunsen burner safely and use the yellow flame when not in use.

Getting started

Before doing the investigation, practise transferring different amounts of water from one test-tube to another. Try transferring $1\,cm^3$, $2\,cm^3$, and $3\,cm^3$ from one test-tube to a beaker that is placed on top of a measuring balance. $1\,cm^3$ is equal to $1\,g$ so you should be able to see how well you were able to transfer the required amount.

Method

1 Prepare a water-bath in the glass beaker using a Bunsen burner, tripod, gauze mat and heat mat.

2 Heat the water almost to boiling point before lowering the heat to keep the water hot.

> **TIP**
>
> The water is almost at boiling point when it is bubbling vigorously.

3 Label the test-tubes with the marker pen (A, B, C and D) and place the test-tubes in the test-tube rack.

4 Using a pipette, add $5\,cm^3$ of the 2% starch solution to each test-tube.

5 Use a different pipette to add $2\,cm^3$ of the amylase solution to tubes B and D. Gently shake the tubes to mix the contents together and leave for 5 minutes.

6 Add 2–3 drops of iodine solution to test-tubes A and B.

7 Use the third pipette to add $3\,cm^3$ of Benedict's solution to test-tubes C and D and place both of these test-tubes in the water-bath for 5 minutes.

8 Observe the results.

Recording data

1 Record your results in the table.

Test-tube	Solutions added	Testing agent used	Colour change
A			
B			
C			
D			

Analysis

2   Suggest a reason for the colour change in test-tube D.

....

3   Identify the nutrient that must be present in test-tube D.

....

4   Describe the colour change in test-tube B.

....

5   Explain the role of amylase in the investigation.

....

....

....

Evaluation

6   Arun repeats this experiment, but he accidentally boils the amylase in the water-bath. Predict what effect boiling the amylase will have on Arun's results by completing the table below.

Test-tube	Solutions added	Testing agent used	Colour change
A			
B			
C			
D			

Practical investigation 5.2:
Effect of temperature on enzyme activity

KEY WORDS

dependent variable: the variable that you measure, as you collect your results

enzyme activity: the rate at which an enzyme works

enzymes: proteins that are involved in all metabolic reactions, where they function as biological catalysts

independent variable: the variable that you manipulate in an investigation

IN THIS INVESTIGATION YOU WILL:

- investigate how different temperatures affect the activity of an enzyme

- apply the effect of temperature on enzyme activity to your knowledge of enzyme structure.

YOU WILL NEED:

- iodine solution   • test-tube × 8   • 2% starch solution
- 5% amylase solution   • marker pen   • pipette × 2   • test-tube rack
- stopwatch   • kettle   • 250 cm³ glass beaker × 4   • thermometer
- safety spectacles   • ice cubes or ice packs.

Safety

- Wash hands after contact with iodine.

- Take care when handling the kettle and the hot water.

Getting started

The independent variable that you are going to change is the temperature. Can you suggest a range of sensible temperatures that could be used?

Method

1   Label the test-tubes 1–8 and place in the test-tube rack(s).

2   Place $5\,cm^3$ of the 2% starch solution into test-tubes 1, 3, 5 and 7.

3   Add 3 drops of iodine solution to test-tubes 1, 3, 5 and 7.

4   Use a second pipette to add $1\,cm^3$ of the 5% amylase to test-tubes 2, 4, 6 and 8.

5   Prepare a water-bath in each of the $250\,cm^3$ glass beakers as follows:

   - ice and water at approximately 10 °C

   - room-temperature water at approximately 20–25 °C

   - water from hot tap (or combined with part-boiled water) at approximately 35–40 °C

   - partially boiled water from the kettle at around 70 °C.

6   Place test-tubes 1 and 2 into the cold water-bath, test-tubes 3 and 4 into the room-temperature water-bath, test-tubes 5 and 6 into the warm water-bath and test-tubes 7 and 8 into the hot water-bath.

7   Leave for 5–10 minutes for the solutions inside the test-tube to match the temperature of the water-bath. You may add more ice cubes or hot water to the water-baths if the temperature is changing.

8   Pour the amylase solution from test-tube 2 into test-tube 1, gently shake to mix the contents, return to the water-bath, and start the stopwatch.

9   Observe and record the time taken for the blue-black colour to disappear and the solution to become colourless.

10   Repeat steps 8–9 for each of the water-baths, using the amylase from test-tubes 4, 6 and 8 respectively.

TIP

The most difficult part of this investigation is controlling the temperature of your water-baths. Work together in teams to ensure that you are monitoring the temperature and then use ice or hot water to keep the water as close to the temperature that you require.

Recording data

1 Construct a table that will show the following for test-tubes 1, 3, 5 and 7:
- the temperature of the water-bath
- the time taken for the test-tubes to become colourless.

> **TIP**
>
> A good table will include suitable units in the headings.

Handling data

2 Construct a line graph to show the results of your investigation. Your graph should include:
- axes drawn using a pencil and ruler
- axes labelled with correct units
- points plotted using a sharp pencil
- points joined by straight lines that do not extend past the final point.

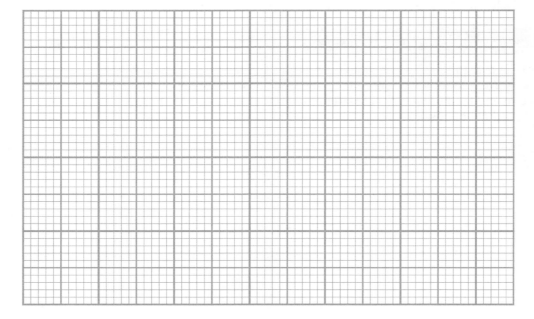

Analysis

3 Determine the temperature at which the reaction happened the fastest.

....

4 Describe the effect of temperature on the rate of reaction of amylase in your investigation.

....

....

5 Explain what happened to the structure of the enzyme to cause the results you saw at 70 °C.

....

....

....

Evaluation

6 Suggest a range of temperatures that you could use to improve this investigation.

....

7 Suggest how the reliability of the investigation could be improved.

....

....

....

....

REFLECTION

The method involves a lot of steps that must be managed at the same time. How did you manage that? How could you amend the method in future, to help you follow the instructions successfully?

....

....

Practical investigation 5.3: Effect of hydrogen peroxide concentration on the activity of catalase

KEY WORD

catalase: an enzyme that catalyses the breakdown of hydrogen peroxide to water and oxygen

IN THIS INVESTIGATION YOU WILL:

- investigate the effect of different concentrations of hydrogen peroxide on the activity of catalase.

YOU WILL NEED:

- large container / water-bath filled with water • measuring cylinder • delivery tube
- bung with two openings:
  - one of the openings will be connected to a syringe of puréed potato
  - the second opening will connect to the delivery tube
- conical flask • hydrogen peroxide solution at 20%, 40% and 60% stock concentration
- stopwatch • safety spectacles • 10 cm³ puréed potato, which contains catalase.

Safety

Wash your hands after the investigation.

Getting started

This investigation involves a complex setup of apparatus. Try setting the apparatus up without the water before attempting to do the experiment properly.

Method

1   Set up the equipment as shown in Figure 5.1. You will need to invert a measuring cylinder full of water into the main water-bath. Then place the delivery tube into the cylinder while connected to the conical flask.

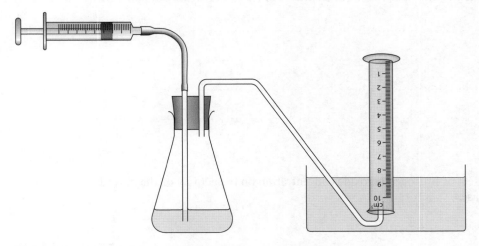

Figure 5.1: Setup of equipment including inverted measuring cylinder.

2   Use the syringe to insert the puréed potato containing the catalase into the hydrogen peroxide (60% stock concentration) and start the stopwatch immediately.

3   Every 30 seconds, measure the volume of oxygen that is in the measuring cylinder by observing the area without water at the top of the cylinder. As the cylinder has a scale, you will be able to measure the volume.

4   After 270 seconds, stop recording and clean each piece of equipment.

5   Repeat steps 1–4 for the following concentrations of hydrogen peroxide:
   *   40%
   *   20%
   *   0%

Recording data

1   Complete the headings of the table below before recording your results in the table.

	0	30	60	90	120	150	180	210	240	270
60										
40										
20										
0										

Handling data

2 The rate of reaction can be compared for each concentration by using the formula:

rate of reaction = amount of oxygen collected / time taken

Use this formula to calculate the rate of reaction for each concentration of hydrogen peroxide.

60% ....

40% ....

20% ....

0% ....

Analysis

3 Describe and explain the effect of hydrogen peroxide concentration on the activity of the puréed potato containing the catalase.

....

....

....

Evaluation

4 Suggest why the use of a 0% hydrogen peroxide concentration improved the investigation.

....

....

....

REFLECTION

The investigation is time-consuming. Were you able to manage your time so that the data was collected within your lesson? If not, how could you have managed your time better?

....

....

EXAM-STYLE QUESTIONS

1   An investigation took place that measured the activity of catalase with different concentrations of hydrogen peroxide.

a   **State** three possible variables that would need to be controlled to ensure a valid result.

....

....

.... [3]

b   **Sketch** a graph for each of the following:

i   The effect of temperature on enzyme activity

[1]

ii   The effect of pH on enzyme activity

[1]

iii The effect of substrate concentration on enzyme activity.

[1]

[Total: 6]

COMMAND WORDS

state: express in clear terms

sketch: make a simple freehand drawing showing the key features, taking care over proportions

CONTINUED

2   A student measures the time taken for starch to be broken down by amylase and records their answers as shown in the table below.

Temperature /°C	Time taken for starch to be broken down/s			
	Attempt 1	Attempt 2	Attempt 3	Average
10	250	240	280	
20	240	240	271	
30	65	55	63	
40	72	70	69	
50	110	120	131	
60	247	278	271	
70	300	301	312	

Use the information in the table to answer the questions that follow.

a   Complete the final column by calculating the average time taken for starch to broken down at each temperature.   [1]

b   Draw a graph to show the relationship between temperature and the time taken to break down starch.

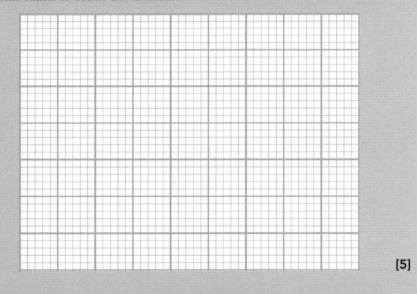

[5]

c   With reference to your graph, **describe** what happens to the time taken to break down starch at different temperatures.   [3]

[Total: 9]

COMMAND WORD

describe: state the points of a topic / give characteristics and main features

> Chapter 6

Plant nutrition

THE INVESTIGATIONS IN THIS CHAPTER WILL:

- enable you to observe the underside of a leaf and make a biological drawing of stomata
- help you to understand how the different colours of light affect the rate of photosynthesis.

Practical investigation 6.1: Epidermal peels

KEY WORD

stomata (singular: **stoma**): openings in the surface of a leaf, most commonly in the lower surface; they are surrounded by pairs of guard cells, which control whether the stomata are open or closed

IN THIS INVESTIGATION YOU WILL:

- observe the epidermal layer of a leaf and make a biological drawing of what you see
- use your knowledge of the stomata to explain when they are open or closed.

YOU WILL NEED:

- microscope • clear nail varnish • leaves (at least 2) • microscope slide
- methylene blue • coverslip • forceps • paper towel.

Safety

Wash hands after handling leaves.

Getting started

In this investigation you will be viewing the underside of a leaf with a microscope. Describe what you expect to see. Do you think the underside of the leaf would look different at certain times of the day? Why do you think this?

Method

1   Set up the microscope.

2   Apply a thin layer of nail varnish to the underside of the leaves, taking care to avoid covering the veins (this will make it easier to remove later).

3   Allow the nail varnish to dry.

> **TIP**
>
> You could use a hairdryer or radiator to make your nail varnish dry more quickly.

4   Peel the nail varnish from the back of the leaf. This can be done by cracking the leaf near the edge of the varnish and it should peel off easily with forceps.

5   Place the varnish onto a microscope slide.

> **TIP**
>
> Make sure that your varnish specimen is as flat as possible so that you can clearly see the stomata that are present on your specimen.

6   Add a drop of methylene blue.

7   Absorb any excess methylene blue with a paper towel.

8   Lower a coverslip at 45 degrees onto the stained nail varnish, as shown in Figure 6.1.

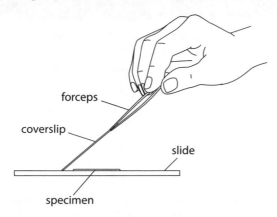

Figure 6.1: Technique to lower coverslip onto specimen.

9   View under the microscope at different magnifications until you can see a number of stomata through the lens.

Recording data

1   Make a biological drawing of what you see through the lens. Record the magnification and label any parts of the leaf that you can identify.

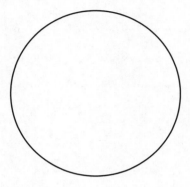

Magnification: ....

Analysis

2   Count the number of stomata that you can see. How many are open and how many are closed?

....

3   Explain why the stomata were open or closed. You will need to know when and where the leaves were collected from.

....

....

....

> **TIP**
>
> Think about whether the leaves were collected fresh and whether their location had sunlight. Will this make a difference to the stomata being open or closed?

Evaluation

4   Design a method that will allow you to compare the number of stomata that are open and closed in leaves from different locations, or in different conditions. Make sure that you control all of the other variables as much as possible.

....

....

....

....

....

....

REFLECTION

How did this investigation help with your understanding of the role of stomata in photosynthesis?

....

....

Practical investigation 6.2: Effect of the light as a limiting factor on the rate of photosynthesis

KEY WORDS

inverting: turning an object upside down

limiting factor: a factor that is in short supply, which stops an activity (such as photosynthesis) happening at a faster rate

photosynthesis: the process by which plants synthesise carbohydrates from raw materials using energy from light

IN THIS INVESTIGATION YOU WILL:

•   investigate how the different colours of light (different environmental conditions) affect the rate of photosynthesis in an aquatic plant.

YOU WILL NEED:

- aquatic plant (such as *Elodea*)   • light source (such as a lamp)   • water
- 1 metre ruler   • stopwatch   • green, red and blue-coloured filter paper   • elastic bands
- boiling tubes   • large glass beaker   • boss clamp and stand   • safety spectacles.

Safety

The lamp will get very hot so must be handled with care.

Getting started

Before attempting the first trial, practise inverting a boiling tube of water into the glass beaker. It can be a tricky manoeuvre so it's better to get it right before you put the *Elodea* into the boiling tube.

Method

1   Wrap a blue-coloured filter around the boiling tube with the elastic bands.

2   Prepare the *Elodea* in advance by cutting it to be shorter than the length of the boiling tube.

3   Set up a metre ruler next to the large glass beaker.

4   Fill the glass beaker with water to approximately half full.

5   Fill the boiling tube with water.

6   Set up the lamp 20 cm away from the glass beaker and turn on the lamp.

7   Place the *Elodea* in the boiling tube.

8 Using the boss clamp and stand, invert the boiling tube containing the *Elodea* and water into the glass beaker, as shown in Figure 6.2.

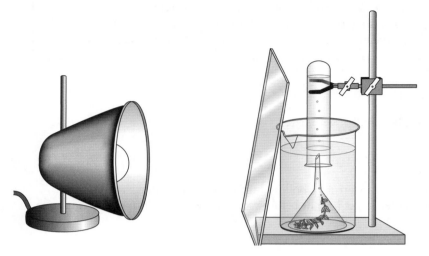

Figure 6.2: Apparatus setup of inverted boiling tube and *Elodea*.

9 Start the stopwatch.

10 Record how many bubbles of oxygen are produced in three minutes.

11 Repeat steps 1–10 with the different coloured filters.

12 If you have time, you can repeat the investigation more than once.

Recording data

1 Record your data into the table below. Extra columns have been added for you to do repeats.

Colour of filter	Number of oxygen bubbles produced			
	1	2	3	Average
Green				
Red				
Blue				

Handling data

2   If you have taken more than one reading for each filter, calculate the average for each one. Complete the final column of the table.

....

....

....

> **TIP**
>
> If you do not have time to take three readings, you can share results with another group and take an average.

Analysis

3   State what you are looking for to determine which colour of light allowed the maximum rate of photosynthesis.

....

4   Rank the results in order of which colour of light allowed the most photosynthesis to happen.

....

....

5   State the limiting factor that was investigated.

....

Evaluation

6   Suggest how this investigation could be adapted to compare the intensity of each colour of light.

....

....

....

EXAM-STYLE QUESTIONS

1 Variegated leaves contain parts that are green and have plenty of chlorophyll. Some parts of the leaf are white and have no chlorophyll.

a Construct a method that would allow you to test for the presence of starch in variegated leaves.

....

....

....

....

....

....

....

....

....

.... [6]

b Based on the description of variegated leaves, **suggest** what you would expect to observe after you have carried out the starch test.

....

....

....

.... [2]

COMMAND WORD

suggest: apply knowledge and understanding to situations where there are a range of valid responses in order to make proposals / put forward considerations

CONTINUED

c **Explain** why you would expect to see the results that you predicted in part **b**.

....

....

....

....

.... [2]

d **State** the balanced chemical equation for photosynthesis.

....

....

.... [3]

e Draw and label a leaf to show how the leaf is adapted for photosynthesis.

[3]

[Total: 16]

explain: set out purposes or reasons / make the relationships between things evident / provide why and/or how and support with relevant evidence

state: express in clear terms

Chapter 7

Human nutrition

THE INVESTIGATIONS IN THIS CHAPTER WILL:

- develop your understanding of the energy content of different food groups
- demonstrate how different substances can affect your teeth.

Practical investigation 7.1: Energy from food

KEY WORDS

joules: unit for measuring energy

specific heat capacity of water: energy required to heat 1 g of water by 1 °C

IN THIS INVESTIGATION YOU WILL:

- investigate the different energy contents of a range of foods
- evaluate your method and plan a second investigation.

YOU WILL NEED:

- Bunsen burner • boss clamp and stand • boiling tube × 4 • thermometer
- heat mat • water • mounted needle • samples of food.

Safety

- Remove ties and tie hair back if long.
- Beware of the hot objects; do not touch the hot needle or any part of the Bunsen apparatus.

Getting started

This investigation requires you to handle a hot boiling tube with confidence. Set up the boss clamp and stand with a boiling tube filled with cold water. Practise the insertion and removal of the boiling tube. Next time you do this will be in the presence of a hot Bunsen flame.

Method

1   Set up the boiling tube and clamp stand as shown in Figure 7.1.

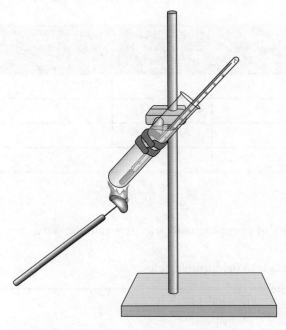

Figure 7.1: Apparatus setup to measure energy content of food.

2   Measure 14 cm³ of water and pour into the boiling tube.

3   Turn on the Bunsen burner and heat the end of the mounted needle for a few seconds until the needle glows red.

4   Mount your food sample onto the mounted needle, taking extra care not to burn or spike yourself with the red-hot needle.

5   Record the starting temperature of the water in the boiling tube.

6   Heat the food in the Bunsen flame until the food begins to burn.

7   Place the burning food under the boiling tube until the food no longer burns.

> **TIP**
>
> Keep the Bunsen burner away from the boiling tube so as not to directly heat the water from the Bunsen burner itself.

8   Record the final temperature of the water.

9   Repeat steps 2–7 with three other food samples.

Recording data

1 Record your data in the table below. Note that you will not complete the final column until the next section.

Food sample	Temperature of the water /°C			Energy transferred /J
	start	end	change	

Handling data

2 Follow the steps to calculate the quantity of energy actually transferred to the water from the food.

   a For each food sample, input the data into the formula below:

$$Q = mc\,\Delta T$$

or

$$\text{energy}/\text{J} = \text{mass of water}/\text{g} \times 4.2\ (\text{J/g °C}) \times \text{temperature change}/°\text{C}$$

Q is the heat energy transferred (in joules).
m is the mass of the water.
c is the specific heat capacity of water (4.2 J/g °C).
ΔT is the temperature change of the water in degrees Celsius.

   b Enter your values into the table.

TIPS

Remember that 1 cm³ of water is equal to 1 g.

Always makes sure that you are using the correct units, especially for energy, mass and specific heat capacity.

Analysis

3 **a** State which food had the highest energy content in your investigation.

....

b Explain how you know that this food had the highest energy content in your investigation.

....

....

....

Evaluation

4 Explain how you controlled the variables for this investigation. Which ones were controlled best to ensure repeatability?

....

....

REFLECTION

Which variables do you think could have been controlled better? How could you improve the method to accommodate these?

....

....

....

Practical investigation 7.2: Modelling enamel on teeth

KEY WORD

enamel: the very strong material that covers the surface of a tooth

IN THIS INVESTIGATION YOU WILL:

- compare how different substances affect eggs

- relate your observations to how different substances affect your teeth.

YOU WILL NEED:

- hardboiled egg with shell still intact × 3   • jar with screw-on lid × 3
- vinegar   • fluoride mouthwash   • marker pen   • stopwatch.

Safety

Do not ingest any of the substances or eggs.

Getting started

Think about the protective layer of enamel on your teeth. Which substances or solutions do you think will do the most damage to that enamel? Can you think of a way that you could test your ideas?

Method

1   Label your jars with your initials.

2   Place an egg in each of the jars.

3   Cover one of the eggs with vinegar and screw the lid on top of the jar.

4   Cover the second egg with fluoride mouthwash and screw the lid on top of the jar.

5   Cover the third egg with a solution of your choice (such as water or fizzy drink).

6   Leave the eggs for at least 24 hours, or until your next lesson.

7   Remove the eggs from the jar and dispose of the solution left inside.

8   Observe the eggs and sketch a diagram to show the difference in the eggs in the Recording data section.

9   Squeeze the eggs gently and observe the difference in how they feel.

Recording data

1 Sketch a diagram of the eggs in the space below.

2 Describe the differences between the eggs that were placed in the different solutions.

....

....

....

Analysis

3 The eggshell represents the enamel of your teeth. Scientists often use models like this to show their understanding. Discuss how your teeth are affected by fizzy drinks.

....

....

....

Evaluation

4 Did you measure the amount of each solution that you put in? Did all of the eggs come from the same source? How might these factors affect the validity of your results?

....

....

....

5 Suggest why it was not appropriate to do the investigation using real teeth.

....

....

....

EXAM-STYLE QUESTIONS

1 A student investigates the energy content of one of her favourite snacks. The student records that a 30 g mass of water is heated from 24 °C to 51 °C.

    a Knowing that the specific heat capacity of water is 4.2 J/g °C and using the appropriate formula, **calculate** the energy transferred from the food to the water.

....

....

....

.... **[3]**

    b **Suggest** two safety precautions that the student should take when investigating the energy content of food.

....

.... **[2]**

    c List the seven types of nutrient that humans require in their balanced diet.

....

....

.... **[1]**

    d For each of the nutrients listed in part **c**, **state** a food in which you can find that nutrient.

....

....

....

....

.... **[7]**

[Total: 13]

COMMAND WORDS

calculate: work out from given facts, figures or information

suggest: apply knowledge and understanding to situations where there are a range of valid responses in order to make proposals / put forward considerations

COMMAND WORD

state: express in clear terms

Chapter 8

Transport in plants

THE INVESTIGATIONS IN THIS CHAPTER WILL:

- allow you to observe how the rate of water moving through a plant can be changed
- identify the product of transpiration
- help you to plan an investigation into how different factors can affect the rate of transpiration.

Practical investigation 8.1: The effect of temperature on transpiration

KEY WORDS

transpiration: the loss of water vapour from leaves

xylem: a plant tissue made up of dead, empty cells joined end to end; it transports water and mineral ions and helps to support the plant

IN THIS INVESTIGATION YOU WILL:

measure how temperature can affect how quickly water can move through the xylem of a celery stem.

YOU WILL NEED:

- celery stem × 3 • food colouring / dye • scalpel or knife
- 250 cm³ glass beaker × 3 • ice to fill a 250 cm³ beaker • kettle
- thermometer • stopwatch / clock × 3 • paper towels • tap water.

Safety

- Wash your hands after handling the plants and dyes.
- Take care when using hot water.

Getting started

The investigation requires three celery stems and three beakers. Read the method and think about why this is important.

Method

1   Cut each piece of celery stem to 10 cm.

2   Prepare a 250 cm³ beaker with 100 cm³ tap water and several drops of food colouring. Record the temperature of the water in the table in the Recording data section.

3   Prepare a second 250 cm³ beaker with ice, 100 cm³ water and food colouring. Record the temperature of the water in the table.

4   Prepare a third 250 cm³ beaker with 100 cm³ of recently boiled water from the kettle and food colouring. Record the temperature of the water in the table.

5   Place one piece of celery into each of the three different beakers at the same time.

6   After 10 minutes, remove the three pieces of celery from the beakers and place onto a paper towel.

7   Use the scalpel to cut the celery as shown in Figure 8.1. Keep cutting until you find where the coloured water has travelled to.

Figure 8.1: How to slice the celery to observe the movement of the dye.

> **TIP**
>
> Slice the celery thinly so that you can see more accurately where the water has travelled to.

8   Record the length of the remaining celery in the table.

Recording data

1   Record your results in this table.

Celery	Temperature of water / °C	Distance that the water had travelled / mm
1		
2		
3		

Handling data

2   Identify at which of the temperatures the water travelled the furthest through the stem.

....

Analysis

3   Calculate the difference between the smallest distance travelled and the greatest distance travelled through the stem.

....

....

4   State the name of the structure that your coloured water travelled through in the stem.

....

Evaluation

5   You used three different temperatures in this investigation. How many temperatures could you use to improve the quality of this investigation?

....

6   Compare your results to those of other students. Are your results similar? If not, why do you think they are not similar?

....

....

REFLECTION

Describe how this investigation has improved your understanding of how water moves through a plant.

....

....

Practical investigation 8.2: Testing the product of transpiration

KEY WORDS

anhydrous copper sulfate: a copper salt that turns blue in the presence of water

IN THIS INVESTIGATION YOU WILL:

test for and identify the product of transpiration.

YOU WILL NEED:

- any potted plant • clear, polythene bag • string or cable tie
- spatula • anhydrous copper sulfate • pipette.

Safety

- Wear gloves when handling anhydrous copper sulfate.

- Wash hands thoroughly after contact with anhydrous copper sulfate. Anhydrous copper sulfate is a corrosive substance and hands should be washed thoroughly with soap and water for several minutes in the event of contact.

Getting started

Tying the bag in step 1 of the method can be tricky to do. Practise this with a partner to ensure that you are able to do it confidently before carrying out the investigation.

Method

1   Water the soil. Place the transparent bag over the plant and tie the bottom of the bag close to the bottom of the plant with the cable tie or string, as shown in Figure 8.2. Tie it firmly.

Figure 8.2: How to tie a potted plant.

2   Place the plant in direct sunlight for at least 12 hours (this may be overnight but allow the plant to receive as much sunlight as possible in that time).

3   Remove the bag without spilling the contents.

4   The liquid inside the bag should collect in the corner of the bag. Remove some of the liquid with the pipette.

5   Add the solution to the anhydrous copper sulfate and record your results.

Recording data

1   Describe the changes that you see inside the bag.

....

....

2   Describe what happens to the anhydrous copper sulfate when the solution is placed onto it.

....

Analysis

3   Identify the solution that you tested with the anhydrous copper sulfate.

....

4   The solution is collected inside the bag as water vapour cools when it hits the cool surface of the bag. State the name of this process that allows you to collect the solution.

....

Evaluation

5   Outline the design of an investigation to compare the different rates of transpiration of two different plant types.

....

....

....

....

....

....

Practical investigation 8.3: Factors that affect the rate of transpiration

IN THIS INVESTIGATION YOU WILL:

plan an investigation into a factor that affects the rate of transpiration.

YOU WILL NEED:

- potometer   • leafy plant   • ruler   • petroleum jelly.

Safety

Wash hands after handling the plant.

Getting started

A potometer is used to measure the rate of transpiration in a plant. Setting up a potometer is a difficult skill. With the aid of your teacher, practise setting up the potometer and ensure that it works before trying your chosen plant cutting.

Method

1   For this investigation, choose one of the following factors to test:

   a   the surface area of a leaf

   b   the number of stomata of a leaf

2 Before beginning the investigation, record the values for your chosen variable:

a Estimate the total surface area of the leaf (or leaves) that you are using – using $1\,cm^2$ squared paper, draw around the outside of the leaves onto the squared paper (Figure 8.3). Count the number of squares inside the drawing.

> **TIP**
>
> If you have 15 squares in total (including parts of squares), then you have $15\,cm^2$ (1 square is equal to $1\,cm^2$).

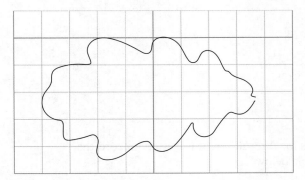

Figure 8.3: Outline drawing of a leaf.

b Estimate the number of stomata that are on the underside of each leaf. You need to repeat the epidermal peels investigation (Investigation 6.1) in this book. Count the number of stomata that you can see on your peel. Extrapolate the number to estimate how many are on the leaf. For example, if the peel contains 10 stomata and the leaf is approximately 15 times bigger than the peel, your estimate will be 150 stomata (10×15).

3 Set up the potometer experiment shown in Figure 8.4.

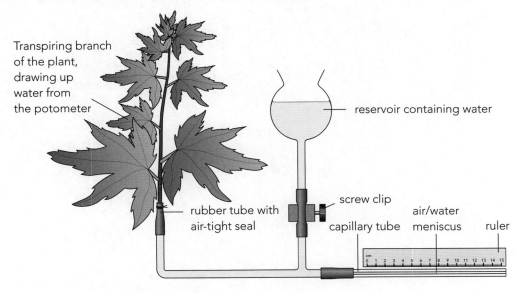

Figure 8.4: Potometer setup.

4 Write out the correct method for observing the rate of transpiration for your chosen leaf.

....

....

....

....

....

....

....

....

....

....

5 Repeat the method for each leaf that you use. Do this for three different leaves and record the surface area or number of stomata in your results table below.

Recording data

1 Construct a table to record your results. Your independent variable should be in the left-hand column and your dependent variable (the distance travelled by the bubble) should be in the right-hand columns. The table should include the time taken for the recordings because you need to know the time taken to calculate the rate. Complete the table with your findings.

Handling data

2 The transpiration rate is the distance travelled by the bubble divided by the time taken. Calculate the transpiration rate for each of your trials.

....

....

....

Analysis

3 Use your results to determine when the transpiration rate was greatest.

....

4 Suggest a reason for your results.

....

....

....

Evaluation

5 Identify the variables that you attempted to control. Explain why these variables had to be controlled.

....

....

....

....

REFLECTION

How could you improve your method so that you are not estimating the surface area or number of stomata?

....

....

EXAM-STYLE QUESTIONS

1 Two students measured the rate of transpiration using a potometer. The students used different leaves from the same plant and a reservoir was provided to allow the refilling of water into the potometer. The investigation ran for approximately one hour, during which time the classroom heating was turned on and off at different times.

a **State** two variables that should be kept the same.

....

.... [2]

b The table below shows the transpiration rate of the leaves used in the investigation.

Leaf	Distance moved by air bubble / mm				Transpiration rate / mm / minute
	1	2	3	Average	
1	120	101	72		
2	109	115	154		
3	70	61	80		
darkness	0	1	1		

i **Calculate** the average distance moved by the bubble in each leaf. Record your answer into the table. [1]

ii Calculate the transpiration rate for each leaf. Record your answer into the table. [2]

c **Identify** a possible source of error in the method and suggest an improvement.

....

....

....

.... [2]

d **Suggest** why the amount of water taken in by the plant might not be the same as the amount of water lost by the plant via transpiration.

....

.... [1]

[Total: 8]

Transport in animals

Practical investigation 9.1: Dissecting a heart

KEY WORDS

aorta: the largest artery in the body, which receives oxygenated blood from the left ventricle and delivers it to the body organs

dissect: dissecting an animal (or plant) to observe internal parts

pulmonary veins: the veins that carry oxygenated blood from the lungs to the left atrium of the heart

IN THIS INVESTIGATION YOU WILL:

- dissect and draw the heart of an animal
- identify the different structures of the heart
- evaluate the safety precautions taken during the investigation.

YOU WILL NEED:

- animal heart • scalpel • latex / rubber gloves • white tile • paper towels
- water • pipette or syringe • forceps • safety spectacles • mounted needle
- surgical scissors • apron.

Safety

- Wear safety spectacles, gloves and apron.
- Wash hands and surfaces after completion of the investigation. Your teacher will ensure that the surfaces are cleaned with disinfectant.
- Do not eat or drink in the laboratory.
- Take care when handling and using the scalpel, scissors and needles.

Getting started

This investigation requires the use of dissection kits and a calm hand. Discuss with your partner what would make your dissection tools good at their function. Why is it important that you are comfortable with using the sharp tools for this investigation?

Method

1   Prepare your working area as directed by your teacher. You should have paper towels under and around your white tile for cutting (if you are not working in a dissection tray or similar container).

2   Put on the gloves, (optional) apron, and safety spectacles.

3   Examine the heart to identify the major parts such as the major blood vessels and the ventricles. The left-hand side of the heart will feel firmer than the right-hand side as it is more muscular.

4   Place the heart on the table/tile/dissection tray so that it is lying flat.

5   Make a longitudinal cut (with the scalpel or scissors) along the side of the heart, slicing carefully through to the opposite side – but do *not* cut all the way through. Use the mounted needle to keep the heart in place.

> **TIP**
>
> Imagine that you are trying to open the heart like a book. Think about where the opening of a book is and how the book opens out. You should aim to make a cut that allows you to open the heart like the book.
>
>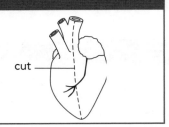

6   Observe the parts of the heart and make a large drawing of the heart in the Recording data section.

7   When you have finished, clear away all materials and equipment as directed by the safety instructions and your teacher.

Recording data

1   In the space below, make a large drawing of your cross section of the heart. Label as many different parts of the heart as you can observe. You may be able to see some, or all, of the following parts: aorta, pulmonary vein, atrial wall, valve tendons, ventricle wall, valve flaps.

Evaluation

2   For each of the following safety precautions, outline why they were taken for this investigation.

   a   Wearing gloves and apron

   ....

   ....

   b   Washing hands

   ....

   ....

   c   Cleaning the surface with disinfectant

   ....

   ....

   d   Not eating or drinking in the laboratory

   ....

   ....

REFLECTION

Discuss with your lab partner how easy or difficult you found it to complete the dissection. Imagine you want to be a surgeon. Discuss the characteristics that a surgeon should have when operating on real people.

Practical investigation 9.2:
Effect of yoga on human heart rate

IN THIS INVESTIGATION YOU WILL:

- investigate how yoga affects the heart rate of humans
- suggest how your findings can help athletes or sports people.

YOU WILL NEED:

- access to yoga techniques (book / leaflet / website) • stopwatch / clock
- suitable area to carry out the yoga techniques.

Safety

Be aware of fitness and ability when selecting people / classmates to carry out all the activities.

Getting started

Two important skills are required for this investigation: yoga moves and measuring your pulse. Practise the yoga moves that you have chosen to ensure that you can do them. You will also need to practise recording your pulse. Place your index and middle finger on the underside of your wrist, below the base of the thumb and with the flat part of your fingers, press firmly. Ensure you are able to feel and count your pulse.

Method

1   Remain at rest for at least one minute.

2   Measure your pulse on your wrist or your neck for 30 seconds. Your teacher will demonstrate how to do this. Count the number of beats in 30 seconds, multiply by two to get your heart rate per minute.

3   Carry out the yoga techniques for five minutes. If you are unsure of which ones to do, search on the internet for the following poses and do each pose for one minute.

     a   Mountain pose

     b   Triangle

     c   Tree

     d   Warrior

     e   Child's pose

4   Record your pulse again. Use the same method that you used in step 2.

5   Repeat steps 1–4 with the different members of your group / class.

Recording data

1   Complete the table with your results on the effect of yoga on heart rate.

Group member	Heart rate before	Heart rate after yoga	Heart rate change
1			
2			
3			
4			
5			

Handling data

2   Complete the table by including the units in the headings.

3   Calculate the difference in heart rate for each person. Complete the final column with your results.

4   Calculate the average change in heart rate for the members of your group.

....

....

....

> **TIP**
>
> The average is calculated by adding together the results and dividing the total by the number of results. For example, if the average change in heart rates for 4 people are: −8, −7, −2, and 0, then the average = (−8 + −7 + −2 + 0) / 4, which would be −4.25.

Analysis

5 Describe the effect that doing yoga had on the average heart rate of the group.

....

....

....

6 Suggest why the change in heart rate might be useful for a sportsperson or athlete.

....

....

....

Evaluation

7 You measured your heart rate by counting your pulse manually. Suggest how you can improve the accuracy of this method.

....

....

8 Consider the members of your group that took part. What differences do they have that might affect the results of your investigation?

....

....

REFLECTION

Think about what you learnt from this investigation. Which variables do you think could have been controlled better? Evaluate how you could improve the method to better control these variables.

....

....

....

Practical investigation 9.3:
Effect of treadmill speeds on heart rate

IN THIS INVESTIGATION YOU WILL:

- investigate the relationship between the running speed of a treadmill and the heart rate of the person using the treadmill

- plot a graph to show the relationship between exercising at different treadmill speeds and human heart rate.

YOU WILL NEED:

- human participants × 3 • heart monitor • treadmill.

TIP

If you do not have access to a heart monitor or a treadmill, consider the following alternatives and adapt the method:

- sports watch or other exercise application

- measure pulse manually (as you did in Investigation 9.2)

- varying levels of exercise (such as walking, jogging, running, sprinting).

Safety

- Only use participants who are fit and healthy.
- Allow participants to stop if they are feeling ill or sick.
- Provide participants with water and keep the room as cool as possible.

Getting started

Trial the treadmill with each participant so that they know how to use the treadmill safely. If measuring your pulse manually, familiarise yourself with the technique that you used in Investigation 9.2.

Method

1   Record the resting heart rate (beats per minute) of the first participant.

2   Participant to exercise at 2 km/h for 30 seconds.

> **TIP**
>
> If your treadmill does not have these speeds, use the speeds available on your treadmill and adjust the table below accordingly.

3   Record the heart rate of the participant.

4   Allow the participant to return to their resting heart rate.

5   Repeat steps 1–4 for treadmill speeds of 4 km/h, 6 km/h, 8 km/h and 10 km/h.

6   Repeat steps 1–5 for each participant.

Recording data

1   Complete the table below with your results.

Treadmill speed/km/h	Heart rate/beats per minute			
	Participant 1	Participant 2	Participant 3	Average
0 (at rest)				
2				
4				
6				
8				
10				

Handling data

2   Calculate the average heart rate of the three participants at each speed and record in the end column of the table.

3   Plot a line graph to show the relationship between the treadmill speed and the average heart rate.

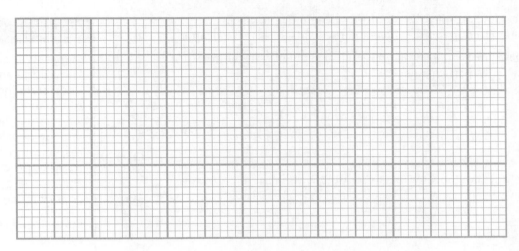

Analysis

4   Describe the effect that increasing the treadmill speed had on the heart rate of the participants.

....

....

5   Explain why the heart rate increased as the speed of the treadmill increased.

....

....

Evaluation

6   The independent variable of the investigation is the different speeds of the treadmill. You used three different participants to gather your data. Identify the variables that you were not able to control in the investigation.

....

....

REFLECTION

How well do you think you were able to explain the process to the participants? Did you ensure that they understood the safety aspects of the investigation?

....

....

EXAM-STYLE QUESTIONS

1 A student is investigating the effect of exercise on human heart rate. He needs to select up to five different participants for his investigation.

    a **Suggest** three variables that the student should try to control when selecting his participants.

....

....

.... [3]

    b **State** why the student wants to control the variables in part **a** for his investigation.

....

.... [1]

    c **Identify** one potential safety precaution associated with the method that would require a safety briefing before doing the exercise.

.... [1]

    d The student notices that the males in his study have a greater change in heart rate than the females. **Describe** a method that could be used to test this hypothesis.

....

....

....

....

....

....

.... [6]

[Total: 11]

COMMAND WORDS

suggest: apply knowledge and understanding to situations where there are a range of valid responses in order to make proposals / put forward considerations

state: express in clear terms

identify: name/ select/recognise

describe: state the points of a topic / give characteristics and main features

Chapter 10

Diseases and immunity

THE INVESTIGATIONS IN THIS CHAPTER WILL:

- help you develop the techniques required to safely culture bacteria

- enable you to observe how different antibacterial mouthwashes affect a culture of bacteria under ideal conditions.

Practical investigation 10.1: Culturing bacteria

KEY WORDS

aseptic technique: technique used to sterilise equipment and destroy all pathogens

inoculating loop: a tool used by biologists to transfer a sample to a Petri dish

Petri dish: shallow dish used to culture microorganisms

sterile: free from microorganisms and pathogens

IN THIS INVESTIGATION YOU WILL:

- become familiar with the techniques required to safely culture bacteria

- become aware of the safety implications of using bacteria in the laboratory.

YOU WILL NEED:

- disinfectant • sterile agar plate (Petri dish) • marker pen • incubator
- Bunsen burner and heat mat • microbe sample in nutrient broth
- inoculating loop • sticky tape.

Safety

- Clean all equipment with disinfectant or similar solution, before and after the investigation.

- Do not open the sealed Petri dish.

- Take care when setting up and using the Bunsen burner.

- Be sure to keep hands well away from the flame when heating using the Bunsen burner.

- Do not eat or drink in the laboratory, even after the investigation has finished. There may be airborne pathogens that you cannot see.
- Do not ingest or inhale the contents of the Petri dish or the bottle of nutrient broth.
- Cover all open wounds or cuts.

Getting started

This investigation requires you to carry out aseptic technique. This involves the following application of streaks to the Petri dish. Do this by using an inoculating loop to streak the dishes. The dishes will not have anything in them, but you will become familiar with the technique before doing so with a hot inoculating loop and a dish full of agar.

Method

1   Wash your hands with soap and water and clean your workbench with the disinfectant.

2   Label the sterile agar plate with your name.

> **TIP**
>
> Label the outer edges of the agar plate so that you can easily observe any changes inside the dish.

3   Turn on your Bunsen burner and use the hotter flame for the next steps.

4   Heat the inoculating loop until it is glowing red-hot. This usually takes a few seconds.

5   Unscrew the bottle of nutrient broth and hold the opening of the bottle in the flame for 2–3 seconds. Be sure to hold the bottle by the bottom and only place the opening of the bottle in the flame.

> **TIP**
>
> It is best to work in pairs to do this stage. One person should hold the bottle ready and one person should control the Bunsen burner flame.

6   Turn off the Bunsen burner.

7   Place the loop into the microbe sample and replace the lid on the bottle.

8   Lift the lid of the Petri dish so that you can just fit the inoculating loop inside. Gently move the loop over the surface of the agar and replace the lid.

9   Seal the Petri dish with the sticky tape as shown in Figure 10.1.

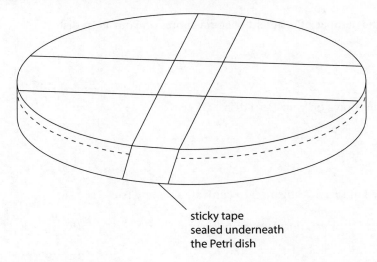

sticky tape
sealed underneath
the Petri dish

Figure 10.1: How to seal a Petri dish safely.

10   Place the dish upside down in the incubator at 25 °C for two days (or until your next lesson).

11   Wash your hands with soap and water and clean your workbench with the disinfectant.

12   **Do not open the sealed Petri dish at any point.**

13   When you get your Petri dish back, observe what has happened inside.

Recording data

1   In the space below, make a labelled drawing of what you can see on your Petri dish after two days.

Handling data

2 Suggest how you could count the number of different bacteria spores on your Petri dish.

....

....

3 Estimate the number of bacteria spores on your Petri dish.

....

Analysis

4 Outline the ideal conditions used in this investigation to cultivate so many bacteria.

....

....

5 Predict what would happen if the Petri dish had been kept at 0 °C for two days.

....

Evaluation

6 Suggest why the workbench was cleaned with disinfectant and why the inoculating loop was held in the flame of the Bunsen burner at the beginning of the investigation.

....

....

7 Suggest why the bacteria should not be stored at 45 °C for two days.

....

....

8 Outline why the Petri dish must not be opened once it has been sealed.

....

....

REFLECTION

This might have been your first time at carrying out aseptic technique. How did you do? Do you think you could improve your technique next time? If so, how would you do this?

....

....

....

Practical investigation 10.2:
Effect of antibacterial mouthwashes on bacteria

KEY WORDS

antibacterial mouthwash: solution used to destroy bacteria in the mouth

IN THIS INVESTIGATION YOU WILL:

- observe how different antibacterial mouthwashes affect a culture of bacteria under ideal conditions
- link your conclusion to how the body is protected from disease and infection.

YOU WILL NEED:

- sterile agar plate (Petri dish) • marker pen • incubator • nutrient broth
- four paper discs ('holes' from a hole punch) • three different antibacterial mouthwashes
- Bunsen burner and heat mat • inoculating loop • sticky tape
- disinfectant • ruler.

Safety

- Clean all equipment with disinfectant or similar solution, before and after the investigation.
- Do not open the sealed Petri dish.
- Take care when setting up and using the Bunsen burner.
- Do not eat or drink in the laboratory.
- Do not ingest or inhale the contents of the Petri dish or the bottle of nutrient broth.
- Cover all open wounds or cuts.

Getting started

What is the purpose of sterilising the equipment before doing the investigation? It might help you to discuss with a partner why we use antibacterial mouthwash, and think about what you expect the mouthwash to do.

Method

1   Wash your hands with soap and water and clean your workbench with the disinfectant.

2   Soak a number of paper discs (use the 'holes' from a hole punch) in each of the three different antibacterial mouthwashes (labelled X, Y, and Z). Soak some additional discs in water as a control.

3   Label the sterile agar plate with your name.

4   Turn on your Bunsen burner and use the hotter flame for the next steps.

5   Heat the inoculating loop until it is glowing red-hot.

6   Unscrew the bottle of nutrient broth and hold the opening of the bottle in the flame for 2–3 seconds.

7   Turn off the Bunsen burner.

8   Place the loop into the microbe sample and replace the lid on the bottle.

9   Lift the lid of the Petri dish so that you can just fit the inoculating loop inside. Gently move the loop over the surface of the agar and replace the lid.

10 Place one of each of the discs (X, Y, Z and the control) onto the agar plate. In the space below, sketch a diagram to record where each disc is located on the agar.

11 Seal the Petri dish with the sticky tape, as shown in Investigation 10.1.

12 Place the dish upside down in the incubator at 25 °C for 48 hours (or until your next lesson).

13 Wash your hands with soap and water and clean your workbench with the disinfectant.

14 **Do not open the sealed Petri dish at any point.**

15 When you get your Petri dish back, observe what has happened inside.

Recording data

1   State the name of the solution that each disc was placed in.

a   Disc X ....

b   Disc Y ....

c   Disc Z ....

d   Control disc ....

2 In the space below, draw and label what happened in your Petri dish after 48 hours in the incubator.

Handling data

3 Without opening the dish, measure the diameter of the clear zone around each disc.

   a Disc X ....

   b Disc Y ....

   c Disc Z ....

   d Control disc ....

Analysis

4 State the name of the disc that had the largest diameter for the clear zone.

....

5 Suggest why this disc had the largest diameter for the clear zone.

....

....

6 Explain how antibacterial mouthwashes protect the body from disease and infection.

....

....

....

Evaluation

7 What was the purpose of the control disc soaked in water for this investigation?

....

....

EXAM-STYLE QUESTIONS

1   Students were given the following hypothesis by their teacher:

"The door handles of the classroom have more bacteria on them than the computer keyboard in the classroom."

a   **Describe** a method that would allow you to test this hypothesis.

....

....

....

....

....

....

....

....

.... [8]

> **COMMAND WORD**
>
> **describe:** state the points of a topic / give characteristics and main features

b   The figure shows a typical bacterium, observed under a microscope at × 12 000 magnification.

i   Measure the length of the cell between the two lines.

.... [1]

ii   **Calculate** the actual length of the bacterium between the two lines.

....

....

....

Answer .... µm **[4]**

[Total: 13]

> **COMMAND WORD**
>
> **calculate:** work out from given facts, figures or information

Chapter 11

Respiration and gas exchange

THE INVESTIGATIONS IN THIS CHAPTER WILL:

- examine respiration under different conditions and the effect on gaseous exchange

- help you to understand the structure of a lung

- provide you with an understanding of how aerobic and anaerobic respiration benefit organisms.

Practical investigation 11.1: Germinating peas

KEY WORD

germination: when a seed develops into a plant

IN THIS INVESTIGATION YOU WILL:

- investigate how much energy is released by germinating peas

- compare your results to a control sample of peas.

YOU WILL NEED:

- vacuum flask × 2
- cotton wool strips
- thermometer × 2
- peas, soaked in cool water for 24 hours
- peas, boiled
- dilute disinfectant
- disposable gloves.

Safety

Wash the peas in disinfectant to prevent bacterial growth.

Getting started

The investigation requires you to secure a thermometer in a flask, using cotton wool as a 'bung'.
Practise the technique required by placing a thermometer and cotton wool bung in the flask.
Does the thermometer and bung remain in place?

Method

1 Wash both sets of peas in the dilute disinfectant.

2 Fill flask A with soaked peas and flask B with boiled peas.

3 Place the thermometer into the middle of the peas and secure this by using the cotton wool to line the inside of the neck of the flask (Figure 11.1).

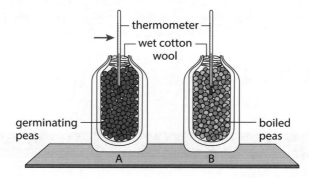

Figure 11.1: Investigating germinating peas.

4 Record the starting temperature of each flask.

5 Place each flask standing as shown in Figure 11.1 and record the change in temperature after 48 hours.

Recording data

1 Construct a table to record the starting temperature and the change in temperature of both sets of peas. Use suitable headings and units in your table.

Analysis

2 Calculate the difference in the temperature change between the boiled peas and the germinating peas.

....

....

3 Suggest a reason for the increase in temperature of the germinating peas.

....

4 How could you use the results of other students to improve the reliability of the investigation?

....

....

Evaluation

5 Explain why the flasks were insulated in the investigation.

....

....

6 Explain the purpose of the boiled peas in the investigation.

....

....

....

....

7 Suggest why the seeds were disinfected at the beginning of the investigation.

....

....

REFLECTION

Investigations like this one are difficult because the results take several days to produce. How could the method be adapted to help you collect the results?

....

....

Practical investigation 11.2: Dissecting a lung

IN THIS INVESTIGATION YOU WILL:

apply your dissection skills to observe the structure of a lung of a mammal.

YOU WILL NEED:

- lung of a mammal
- clear plastic tubing
- dissection tray
- scalpel
- dissection scissors
- disposable gloves
- 250 cm³ beaker, half-filled with water.

Safety

- Wear gloves.

- Wash hands after completion of the investigation.

- Take care using the sharp dissection tools.

- Do not eat or drink in the laboratory. Airborne pathogens may be present after the dissection has been completed.

Getting started

The most dangerous part of this investigation is when inflating the lungs with the tube. It is natural to breathe in before a large sucking action. If you do that, you will certainly take in parts of the lung into your mouth and this would be potentially dangerous for your health. Try using a straw to practise the intake of breath *before* placing your mouth around the straw and blowing outwards.

Method

1 Prepare your dissection area and equipment.

2 Feel the lungs and observe the different features and their size. Discuss the features with your lab partner.

3 Identify the different areas that you can see. You should be able to see the trachea, the C-shaped tracheal rings, the bronchi, the bronchioles, the pleural membrane, and possibly some of the blood vessels that travel to and from the heart.

> ### TIP
>
> Try to follow the pathway of air from an obvious starting point at the top of the trachea, if possible.

4 Insert the plastic tubing down the trachea into one of the lungs.

5 Take a deep breath and blow firmly into the tubing to inflate the lungs. Be careful not to suck.

6 Observe the difference in size of the inflated lung compared to before inflation.

7 Use the dissection tools to remove pieces of lung tissue and examine the structure closely. Make a labelled drawing of your lung specimen in the 'Recording data' section.

8 Place a piece of lung into the beaker of water and observe what happens. Record your observations below.

Recording data

1 Make a labelled drawing of your lung specimen.

2 Describe what happened to the piece of lung that you placed into water.

....

Analysis

3 Suggest why this happened to the lung tissue when placed in water.

....

....

Evaluation

4 Outline how you could compare the difference in size of the inflated lung compared to when it was not inflated.

....

....

5 Suggest what your teacher should do to your work surface to ensure the safety of the next class. Explain your answer.

....

....

Practical investigation 11.3: Repaying the oxygen debt

KEY WORDS

breathing rate: the number of breaths taken per minute

oxygen debt: extra oxygen that is needed after anaerobic respiration has taken place, in order to break down the lactic acid produced

IN THIS INVESTIGATION YOU WILL:

plan an investigation to observe the time required to repay the oxygen debt.

YOU WILL NEED:

- stopwatch • suitable area for your activity.

Safety

- Stop exercise if feeling unwell or dizzy.

- Drink water during and after exercise as required.

- Clear sufficient space for safe exercise with no tripping hazards.

Getting started

Using a stopwatch is a common, but underestimated, skill. How good are you at using stopwatches? Try the following activities to see how 'accurate' you are.

- Try stopping the stopwatch on exactly five seconds (5:00). How close to '00' can you get?

- In a small group, try timing something short. For example, time how long someone can hold their breath and then compare results. Did you all get the same value? If not, how could you improve the accuracy of your stopwatch use?

Method

1   Plan a method that incorporates the following:

   - measuring breathing rate before exercise

   - vigorous exercise that will cause muscles to begin to ache

   - measuring of breathing rate every minute after exercise until breathing rate returns to the resting rate.

   ....

   ....

   ....

   ....

   ....

   ....

   ....

   ....

   ....

   ....

   ....

TIP
Add a step to your method to ensure that the participant can return their breathing rate to 'normal'.

Recording data

2 Construct a table to record:

- your breathing rate at rest

- your breathing rate every minute after exercise

- the number of minutes required to return to the resting breathing rate.

Use appropriate headings and units for your table.

Analysis

3 Plot a line graph to show the change in breathing rate from the resting period to when the rate returns to the resting rate after exercise.

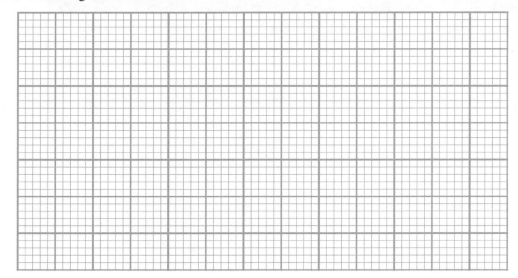

4   Describe the changes in breathing rate from the start to finish of the investigation.

....

....

....

5   Explain why the breathing rate remained higher than the resting breathing rate after the exercise
had finished.

....

....

....

6   State the name of the substance that caused your muscles to ache during the exercise.

....

7   Define what the recovery period is in the investigation.

....

....

Evaluation

8   In your method, how did you ensure that the participants were of similar types?

....

....

9   How would your results have been affected if the participants were of different sexes or
age groups?

....

....

REFLECTION

You designed your own method for this investigation. Evaluate your plan for measuring
the time taken to return to the resting rate. What would you improve if you did the
investigation again?

....

....

....

Practical investigation 11.4: Expired and inspired air

IN THIS INVESTIGATION YOU WILL:

- investigate the differences between expired and inspired air

- use the basic tests for carbon dioxide and oxygen.

YOU WILL NEED:

- thermometer • mirror • boiling tube • plastic straws • paper towel
- limewater • cobalt chloride paper • wooden splint • matches.

Safety

- Be careful when handling the lit splint.

- Be careful not to suck up the limewater into your mouth. Wash your mouth immediately and seek medical attention if you ingest the limewater.

Getting started

It would be easy to accidentally suck in the limewater instead of blowing bubbles into the limewater. Also, it is easy to blow too hard, causing the limewater to spill out. Practise the blowing technique by using a straw placed into normal drinking water.

Method

For each of the steps below, you will need to record your observations. Read the method carefully.

1 Record the temperature of the thermometer. Blow gently onto the thermometer. Record the temperature again.

2 Exhale lightly onto the mirror. Test the vapour by placing the cobalt chloride paper onto the condensation on the mirror. Record your results.

3 Pour limewater into the boiling tube to about a third of the way up. Pierce a paper towel with the straw and use the paper towel as a makeshift lid to the boiling tube. Blow gently through the straw into the limewater for 10–15 seconds and record the change.

4 Light a wooden splint and extinguish the flame but allow it to remain glowing. Exhale lightly onto the glowing splint and record your observations.

TIP

Some of these techniques require you to exhale lightly. Practise doing so before recording the changes. Try to keep your mouth wide open and exhale lightly from the back of the mouth.

Recording data

1   For each of the tests, record your observations in the spaces below.

   a   Blow onto thermometer

   ....

   b   Exhale onto mirror

   ....

   c   Blow into limewater

   ....

   d   Exhale on glowing splint

   ....

Analysis

2   Explain the results for each of the tests.

   a   Blow onto thermometer

   ....

   ....

   b   Exhale onto mirror

   ....

   ....

   c   Blow into limewater

   ....

   ....

   d   Exhale on glowing splint

   ....

   ....

Evaluation

3   The reading on the thermometer is difficult to read. How could you improve the accuracy of
    this reading?

   ....

EXAM-STYLE QUESTIONS

1 A student is relaxing at home and decides that she is going to run on the treadmill as part of an attempt to be fit and healthy. The student has been sitting for 3 minutes but then runs for 7 minutes until the muscles in her legs begin to ache. The student sits down for 4 minutes until her breathing rate returns to normal.

   a **Sketch** a graph to show how the student's breathing rate might change over time.

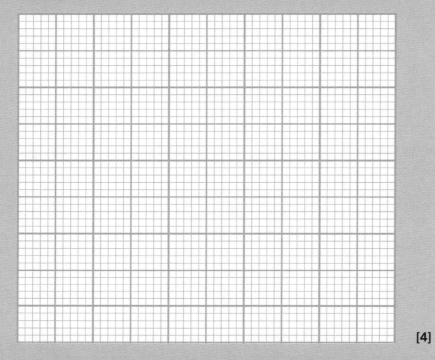

[4]

   b **Describe** the change in breathing rate for the student.

....

.... [2]

   c **Explain** why the student's breathing rate did not return to normal until 4 minutes after she finished exercising.

....

....

.... [4]

COMMAND WORD

sketch: make a simple freehand drawing showing the key features, taking care over proportions

---

COMMAND WORDS

describe: state the points of a topic / give characteristics and main features

explain: set out purposes or reasons / make the relationships between things evident / provide why and/or how and support with relevant evidence

CONTINUED

d   The student's teacher wants to compare the breathing rate before and after exercise. **Suggest** two variables that should be kept constant in the investigation.

....

.... [2]

[Total: 12]

2   A student runs 5 km every morning. Explain how her breathing rate would change during the course of her run.

....

....

....

.... [4]

3   **State** the balanced chemical equation for aerobic respiration.

.... [3]

COMMAND WORDS

suggest: apply knowledge and understanding to situations where there are a range of valid responses in order to make proposals / put forward considerations

state: express in clear terms

> # Chapter 12

Coordination and response

THE INVESTIGATIONS IN THIS CHAPTER WILL:

- investigate how the human body reacts to different stimuli
- link human reaction times to the purpose of voluntary and involuntary reactions
- observe different involuntary human responses.

Practical investigation 12.1: Measuring reaction times

KEY WORDS

reaction time: time taken to respond to a stimulus

IN THIS INVESTIGATION YOU WILL:

- measure your own reaction time
- compare your reaction time to those of your peers.

YOU WILL NEED:

- selection of rulers • table or bench to rest arm on.

Safety

If using a wooden ruler, check that the ruler does not have fragments of wood sticking out that may cause minor cuts or splinters.

Getting started

In this investigation, you will measure the reaction time for catching a ruler. Gather different rulers available in your classroom (such as 15 cm, 30 cm, 50 cm and 1 m). Discuss with your partner which one would be best for measuring the reaction time in the investigation.

Method

1   Work in pairs for this investigation, reversing roles when the method is complete.

2   Student A rests their arm on a table or lab bench with their hand hanging free.

3   Student B places their chosen ruler between the forefinger and thumb of student A. The '0' end of the ruler should be at the bottom, level with the forefinger and thumb.

4   When student B lets go of the ruler (without warning), student A must catch it between their forefinger and thumb.

5   Record the point on the ruler where the ruler was caught by student A.

6   Repeat steps 2–5 three more times.

7   Reverse roles for students A and B and repeat steps 2–6.

Recording data

1   In the space below, plan and draw a table to record the results for you and your partner. Include a column to calculate the mean for the distance caught.

Handling data

2   Use the data in Table 12.1 to calculate the reaction time for you and your partner's mean distance caught.

> **TIP**
>
> For example, if the average distance caught was 31 mm, then your reaction time would be 0.078 s.

Distance /mm	Reaction time/s	Distance /mm	Reaction time/s	Distance /mm	Reaction time/s
10	0.045	140	0.169	270	0.235
20	0.064	150	0.175	280	0.239
30	0.078	160	0.181	290	0.243
40	0.09	170	0.186	300	0.247
50	0.102	180	0.192	310	0.252
60	0.111	190	0.197	320	0.256
70	0.12	200	0.202	330	0.26
80	0.128	210	0.207	340	0.263
90	0.136	220	0.212	350	0.267
100	0.143	230	0.217	360	0.271
110	0.15	240	0.221	370	0.275
120	0.156	250	0.226	380	0.278
130	0.163	260	0.23	390	0.282

Table 12.1: Reaction times for different distances caught.

Your reaction time: ....   Your partner's reaction time: ....

Analysis

3   Did your reaction time (or the distance at which the ruler was caught) improve with practice? Suggest a reason for this.

   ....

   ....

4   Predict how your reaction time might be different if the ruler was touching your hand when it was let go.

   ....

5   Plan and carry out a method to test your answer to Question **4**.

....

....

....

....

Evaluation

6   Identify possible sources of error in the method and suggest ways to reduce these errors.

....

....

....

....

7   Suggest how you could change the method so that you test your reaction time with your hearing only.

....

....

Practical investigation 12.2: Sensitivity test

KEY WORD

sensitivity: the ability to detect and respond to changes in the internal or external environment

IN THIS INVESTIGATION YOU WILL:

- measure the sensitivity of different parts of your body
- suggest why some people have different results to others.

YOU WILL NEED:

piece of wire (or paper clip).

Safety

- Do not press too hard with the wire.
- Do not press the wire on/in the eyes, mouth, inside the nose, ears or any other sensitive area.

Getting started

You are going to be using a paper clip to test the sensitivity of your body. What other methods could you devise that might (safely) test the sensitivity of different body parts? What equipment would you need to do so?

Method

1   Bend a piece of wire (or paper clip) so that the ends are 5 mm apart, as shown in Figure 12.1.

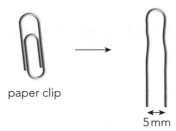

paper clip

5 mm

Figure 12.1: How to bend the paper clip.

> **TIP**
>
> You can use a pencil to help bend the paper clip around to create a uniform shape.

2   With your partner, discuss which parts of the body you will test for sensitivity.

3   Student A looks away or closes their eyes while student B touches the skin with the ends of the wire. Do not hit them or poke them with the wire; just press the wire firmly against the skin. Be respectful of your partner and their preferences.

4   Student A states whether they can feel one or two points of the pin.

5   Test five different areas of the body, using the same amount of force, and record the results in the table below.

6   Student A and student B reverse roles and repeat steps 3–5. Check that the gap between the wires is 5 mm each time.

Recording data

1 Record your results in the table.

Area being tested	Points felt by student A	Points felt by student B

Analysis

2 State the areas that you could feel two points.

....

3 State the areas that you could feel only one point.

....

4 Suggest why you could feel two points in some areas but not in others.

....

5 Compare your results to others in the class. Suggest why some people could feel things differently to others.

....

....

REFLECTION

Consider the ethics of the investigation. What care did you have to take to ensure that your partner was happy to be tested with your paper clip?

....

....

....

Practical investigation 12.3: Human responses

KEY WORDS

response: behaviour that results from a stimulus

stimulus (plural: **stimuli**): change in the environment that can be detected by organisms

IN THIS INVESTIGATION YOU WILL:

- observe involuntary responses of the body when reacting to stimuli.

YOU WILL NEED:

- torch • half-metre ruler • chair • table or bench.

Safety

- Take care when sitting and kneeling on the table and chair.
- Do not tap hard when tapping the knee and the heel. You should not be causing pain to the person being tested.
- Do not press too firmly on your eyelid.

Getting started

Think of different stimuli, such as a flash of light, a sudden sound or a ball coming towards you. What other stimuli to the human body could you observe in the laboratory?

Method

There are five different tests for you to do. Record your observation for each one in the table in the Recording data section.

Test 1

1   Shine a torch briefly in your partner's eye. Record their reaction.

Test 2

2   Sit on the edge of a table or workbench. Sharply tap the point just below the knee with the ruler. Record the reaction of your partner's leg. Figure 12.2 shows you where to hit the knee.

Figure 12.2: How to test the patellar reflex.

Test 3

3   Wave your hand in front of your partner's eyes. Record their reaction, if any.

Test 4

4   Remove your shoes and socks. Have your partner kneel on a chair so that their feet are hanging over the edge of the chair. Tap the back of your partner's heel lightly with the ruler. Record your observation of the reaction.

Test 5

5   Draw a square of approximately $2\,\text{cm}^2$ on plain paper. Press lightly on the upper eyelid of one of your closed eyes for a few seconds. Release your eyelid and try to look at the box on the paper. Record the effect of this.

Recording data

1   Record your observations in the table below.

Stimuli	Reaction
Shine torch in eye	
Tap below the knee	
Wave hand in front of eyes	
Tap back of heel	
Eyelid pressure and focus on box	

Analysis

2   Describe and explain the reaction to each of the stimuli in the table.

....

....

....

....

....

....

....

....

Evaluation

3   Suggest why some students in this investigation might have experienced different reactions.
     For example, some students might not have blinked during Test 3.

....

....

REFLECTION

Discuss with your partner how you could use technology to improve some of
the observations.

EXAM-STYLE QUESTIONS

1   A student investigates the reaction times of his classmates and records his results in the table.

Reaction time / s	Number of students
0.089	2
0.09–0.111	8
0.12–0.136	11
>0.137	3

a   Plot a bar chart of the data in the table.

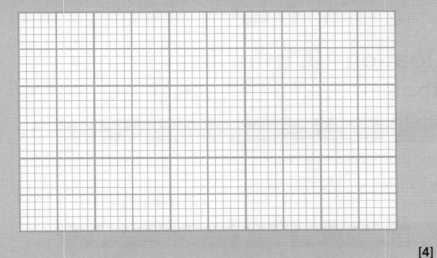

[4]

b   The student tested each person once. **Suggest** how the reliability might be affected by this.

....

.... [2]

c   Draw and label a reflex arc.

[5]

[Total: 11]

COMMAND WORD

suggest: apply knowledge and understanding to situations where there are a range of valid responses in order to make proposals / put forward considerations

> Chapter 13

Excretion and homeostasis

THE INVESTIGATIONS IN THIS CHAPTER WILL:

- examine the structure of the kidney

- model how a body can retain heat energy

- help you to understand how the body remains cool.

Practical investigation 13.1: Kidney dissection

KEY WORDS

cortex: the tissue making up the outer layer in a kidney

medulla: the tissue making up the inner layers in a kidney

IN THIS INVESTIGATION YOU WILL:

- dissect a mammalian kidney

- draw and label your dissected kidney

- calculate the magnification of your drawing.

YOU WILL NEED:

- kidney of a mammal • dissection tray • dissection scissors • scalpel
- safety spectacles • latex gloves (or nitrile if you have a latex allergy) • ruler • balance.

Safety

- Take care when using a scalpel, or scissors.
- Wear gloves and safety spectacles.
- Wash hands afterwards, even if you have been wearing gloves.

Getting started

In the space below, sketch a diagram of what you expect to see inside the kidney. What level of detail will you be able to see in parts like the medulla and the cortex?

Method

1   Prepare your dissection area and collect the equipment that you will need.

2   Examine the external appearance of the kidney. Identify the structures that you can see. These may include the ureter, renal artery and renal vein.

3   Record the mass and the length of the kidney in the Recording data section.

4   Place the kidney on its flat side and place your palm on top of the kidney to hold it steady.

5   Use the scalpel to cut through the kidney from the side until you almost reach the opposite side of the kidney.

> **TIP**
>
> Allow the blade of the scalpel to 'do the work' when dissecting. You should not be pushing hard against the kidney but allowing smooth incisions to slice cleanly through the tissue.

6   You can now open the kidney like a book to reveal the internal structures of the kidney.

7   Make a large, labelled drawing of your kidney in the Recording data section.

Recording data

1   Record the following information:

   a   Mass of kidney: ....

   b   Length of kidney: ....

   c   Labelled drawing of the internal structures of the kidney (in the space below).

Handling data

2   Calculate the magnification of your drawing compared to the kidney that you dissected.
     Give your answer to three significant figures.

     Magnification: ....

Analysis

3   Select one of the internal structures that you can see in the kidney that you dissected.
     Describe the function of your chosen structure.

     ....

     ....

Evaluation

4   Not all of the internal structures of the kidney could be seen with the naked eye.
     Suggest how structures such as the nephrons could be viewed.

     ....

     ....

     ....

Practical investigation 13.2: Controlling body temperature

KEY WORD

thermoregulation: the process that allows the temperature of the body to be maintained

IN THIS INVESTIGATION YOU WILL:

- measure the effects of insulation on the loss of heat energy from a controlled system
- calculate the overall temperature change and the percentage change in temperature.

YOU WILL NEED:

- insulated cup × 4   • different insulating materials   • thermometer
- elastic band × 4   • kettle or hot water source   • stopwatch.

Safety

Take care when handling hot water.

Getting started

Taking the temperature of a solution is something that you do often. However, it is easy to do incorrectly. Practise taking the temperature of some water, making sure that you have stirred the water to ensure an even temperature throughout. The thermometer should not be touching any part of the beaker. Compare your readings with those of your partner. Do you have the same reading?

Method

Plan your investigation with your partner/group and draw a suitable table for recording the data in the Recording data section.

1   Select three of the insulation materials provided and cut them into the same size (by area), large enough to be able to surround the outside and top of the insulated cup.

2   Add hot water from the kettle to a insulated cup.

3   Immediately wrap one of the chosen materials around the cup, covering the top of the cup as well as the sides, securing in place with the elastic band.

4   Penetrate the material with the thermometer and record the starting temperature.

5   Start the stopwatch and leave the water for five minutes.

6   After five minutes, take the end temperature and record it in the table.

7   Repeat steps 2–6 for all of the materials, including one test without any material.

TIP

One person should be ready with the material to secure around the top of the beaker as soon as another person adds the hot water. A third person should then be ready to penetrate the material with the thermometer. Teamwork and being ready are key to not losing heat energy from the water before you start recording.

Recording data

1   In the space below, draw a table to record the starting temperature and the end temperature and the overall temperature change (with units) for the different insulating materials that you investigated.

Handling data

2 Calculate the percentage change in temperature for the material that had the greatest change in temperature. Show your working.

Answer: ....

Analysis

3 Describe the change in temperature for the insulating materials that you tested.

....

....

4 Explain how an insulating layer of material can reduce the loss of heat energy from a system.

....

....

5 The human body reacts to a drop in internal temperature by standing hairs on end to create an insulating layer of air above the skin. Outline how this investigation supports that this action is useful in thermoregulation.

....

....

....

Evaluation

6 Suggest why the insulating materials all had the same surface area.

....

....

7 Suggest how step 2 of the method could be changed to improve the validity of the investigation.

....

....

8 Outline why one test was carried out without using any material at all.

....

....

REFLECTION

Think about the time it took to get the materials and rubber bands onto the beaker. Did this affect your results in any way and what could you do to minimise the effect?

....

....

....

Practical investigation 13.3: Evaporation rates from the skin

KEY WORD

evaporation: when a liquid changes to a gas

IN THIS INVESTIGATION YOU WILL:

- observe how different solutions evaporate at different rates
- relate your observations to how sweating keeps us cool.

YOU WILL NEED:

- thermometer × 3 • test-tube rack or boss clamp × 3 and stand
- cotton wool ball × 3 • water • acetone • pipette • safety spectacles.

Safety

- Acetone is highly flammable, keep away from head and naked flames.
- Wash hands after using acetone and do not ingest it.

Getting started

Spray / splash aftershave, deodorant and water onto your skin. Compare the effects that each one has on your skin.

Method

1 Set up the three thermometers so that they are upside down, using a test-tube rack.

2 Prepare three cotton wool balls of equal size and wrap them around the bulb-end of the thermometer to create a large cotton swab.

3 Record the temperature of each thermometer.

4 Using a pipette, add enough water to soak the first cotton wool ball and record the change in temperature after 30 seconds.

5 Repeat step 4, using the acetone and record the change in temperature after 30 seconds.

6 Record the temperature of the third thermometer. The third thermometer is a control and will not have any solution added.

Recording data

1 Prepare and complete a table to show the change in temperature of each of the three cotton wool balls.

Analysis

2 Describe and explain the change in temperature of the three cotton wool balls.

....

....

3 If you spray perfume or aftershave onto your skin, it feels cold. Use the results from this investigation to explain why this happens.

....

....

4 Suggest how the removal of water in sweat from the skin by evaporation removes heat energy from the skin in order to keep you cool.

....

....

Evaluation

5 Draw a table in the space below to show how you would repeat the investigation to obtain data that are more reliable.

6 The third cotton wool ball was kept dry as a control. Suggest how this helped the investigation.

....

....

REFLECTION

Suggest how you can improve your method by using data loggers.

....

....

EXAM-STYLE QUESTIONS

1 A student records his body temperature at 5-minute intervals for 30 minutes while standing in a cool room. He does not move during the investigation and records his temperature in a table, as shown:

Time/minutes	Temperature/°C
0	37.5
5	37.4
10	37.2
15	37.0
20	36.1
25	35.6
30	35.0

CONTINUED

a Draw a suitable graph to show how the student's body temperature changed over time.

[5]

b **Describe** the change in body temperature for the student.

....

.... [2]

c **Outline** what the thermoregulatory response of the student's body would be during the 30-minute period.

....

....

....

....

.... [5]

d **Define** homeostasis.

....

.... [1]

[Total: 13]

Chapter 14

Reproduction in plants

THE INVESTIGATIONS IN THIS CHAPTER WILL:

- examine the structure of a flower

- investigate the importance of oxygen for successful germination

- observe how temperature can affect the rate of germination.

Practical investigation 14.1: Structure of a flower

KEY WORDS

carpel: the female part of a flower

longitudinal cut: a cut made along the long axis of a structure

sepal: leaf-like structure that forms a ring outside the petals of a flower

stamen: the male part of a flower

IN THIS INVESTIGATION YOU WILL:

observe, measure and draw the structure of a flower from an insect-pollinated flowering plant.

YOU WILL NEED:

- scalpel and cutting board • A4 paper or card and glue / sticky tape
- hand lens • flower • microscope slide • microscope.

Safety

Take care when handling the scalpel.

Getting started

The techniques in this investigation require a delicate touch. Watch a video of how to dissect a flower and observe how careful the person is with their hand movements and incisions.

Method

1   Remove the sepals and the petals of the flower by pulling them downwards in the direction of the stem. Do not discard any of the parts of the flower that you remove.

2   Use the hand lens to examine one of the petals and make a large labelled drawing of the petal in the Recording data section.

3   Remove the stamens by cutting them carefully with the scalpel. Transfer the pollen grains onto a microscope slide and observe them under the microscope. Make a large labelled drawing of a pollen grain in the Recording data section.

> **TIP**
>
> Apply minimal pressure with the scalpel to avoid cutting all the way through the flower.

4   Remove all parts of the flower until just the carpel remains. Make a longitudinal cut to reveal the hollow insides of the carpel. Make a large labelled diagram of the inside of the carpel in the Recording data section.

5   Your teacher may provide you with two different plants. If so, repeat steps 1–4 for the second plant. With your partner, compare the similarities and differences between the two plants.

Recording data

1   Make your labelled drawings in the spaces below.

Drawing of a petal

Drawing of a pollen grain

Drawing of the inside of a carpel

Handling data

2   Take the parts of the flower that you removed or dissected and stick them to a blank piece of A4 paper. Label each part and outline the function of each part that you removed. Your flower posters will make a valuable classroom resource.

Analysis

3   For your drawing of the petal, calculate the magnification of your drawing compared to the actual petal. Show your working.

Magnification: ....

REFLECTION

Compare your dissected flowers to your classmates. Evaluate their dissection of the flower. What did they do well and what could they improve when doing this investigation?

....

....

....

Practical investigation 14.2: Oxygen for germination

KEY WORDS

alkaline pyrogallol: caustic substance that removes oxygen

IN THIS INVESTIGATION YOU WILL:

observe how important oxygen is for germination.

YOU WILL NEED:

- alkaline pyrogallol
- sewing thread to suspend the cotton wool
- water
- bung for boiling tube × 2
- cress seeds on moist cotton wool × 2
- boiling tube × 2.

Safety

- Alkaline pyrogallol is a caustic substance and must be handled *only* by a teacher who has observed the relevant safety precautions for use.

- Do not eat or drink in the laboratory.

Getting started

It is unlikely that you have used alkaline pyrogallol before. Find out what it is and why your teacher is going to demonstrate this investigation instead of you doing it yourself.

Method

This is a teacher demonstration for safety reasons but the method is outlined here for your observation and use.

1 Set up two boiling tubes, A and B, as shown in Figure 14.1.

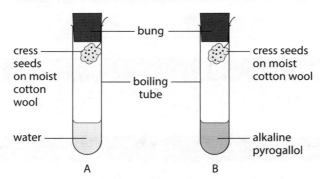

Figure 14.1: Apparatus setup.

2 Alkaline pyrogallol absorbs oxygen. Use this information to make a prediction for what will happen in boiling tube A and B in the Recording data section.

3 Leave the two boiling tubes in a safe place for 48 hours and observe.

4 Record the differences and compare them to your predictions.

Recording data

1 Make your predictions for what will happen in each of the boiling tubes:

a Boiling tube A:

....

....

b Boiling tube B:

....

....

After 48 hours, note your observations for each boiling tube:

c Boiling tube A:

....

....

d Boiling tube B:

....

....

Analysis

2 Describe the differences between the contents of the two boiling tubes.

....

....

3 Alkaline pyrogallol absorbs oxygen. Describe and explain the effect that the absence of oxygen had on the cress seeds.

....

....

Evaluation

4 Outline why boiling tube A contained water.

....

....

5 Alkaline pyrogallol is a caustic substance. State why this investigation had to be carried out by the teacher.

....

....

6 Predict what would happen if the seeds from boiling tube B were removed and placed into boiling tube A for 48 hours.

....

....

REFLECTION

How did your prediction in Question **1** compare to what actually happened when the teacher did the demonstration?

....

....

Practical investigation 14.3: Measuring the effect of temperature on the germination of cress seeds

IN THIS INVESTIGATION YOU WILL:

observe the effect of temperature on the germination of cress seeds.

YOU WILL NEED:

- cress seed × 15   • Petri dish   • thermometer
- cotton wool or paper towels   • access to a refrigerator.

Safety

Wash your hands after handling the seeds.

Getting started

Soaking the cotton wool in this investigation requires a different volume of water, depending on the type, and size, of cotton wool used. Practise soaking your cotton wool to establish the most appropriate volume. Doing this will make your method more valid.

Method

Cress seeds require the following conditions for germination:

- Damp cotton wool or paper towel placed inside a Petri dish.

- The seeds should be kept damp, but not soaked.

- Seedlings will take up to 10–14 days for maximum growth without extra nutrients being provided but you can compare the rate of germination in each lesson during that time.

1   Use this information to plan a method to germinate cress seeds at three different temperatures and to record the rates of germination of the resulting cress seedlings over a period of 14 days.

....

....

....

....

....

....

Allow the seeds to be evenly spread so that they have room for growth.

Recording data

2   Prepare a results table to record the heights of the cress seedlings over the course of your investigation. Include a column in your table to calculate the number of seeds that germinated.

Handling data

3   Calculate the number of seeds that germinated in each of the different temperatures. Use germination (%) = no. of seeds that germinated/no. of seeds in tray × 100.

   a   Number of seeds, temperature A:

   ....

   b   Number of seeds, temperature B:

   ....

   c   Number of seeds, temperature C:

   ....

Analysis

4   Explain the results of your investigation.

   ....

   ....

   ....

   ....

Evaluation

5 Suggest why you might get different results if you used mustard seeds instead of cress seeds.

....

....

REFLECTION

Swap methods with other students. How does your method compare to others?

....

....

EXAM-STYLE QUESTIONS

1

a **State** the name of the part of the flower labelled X in the figure.

.... [1]

b **Describe** the function of the part of the flower labelled X.

....

.... [2]

c State the name of the part of the flower labelled Y.

.... [1]

COMMAND WORDS

state: express in clear terms

describe: state the points of a topic / give characteristics and main features

CONTINUED

d   Make a large labelled drawing of the part of the flower labelled Z.

[5]

e   **Identify** the part of the flower labelled Z and describe its function.

....

.... [2]

[Total: 11]

2   A student investigates the effect of temperature on seed germination.

a   **Suggest** a suitable range of temperatures that the student should use.

.... [2]

b   Suggest how many times the investigation should be repeated for reliable data to be produced.

.... [1]

c   State what safety precautions the student should take for the investigation.

....

.... [1]

d   One of the seeds grows from 4 mm to 11 mm in one day. **Calculate** the percentage change in the growth of the seed.

....

....

.... [3]

[Total: 7]

COMMAND WORDS

identify: name/select/recognise

suggest: apply knowledge and understanding to situations where there are a range of valid responses in order to make proposals / put forward considerations

calculate: work out from given facts, figures or information

Chapter 15

Reproduction in humans

model how the amniotic fluid protects the growing fetus.

Practical investigation 15.1: Protecting the fetus

KEY WORDS

amniotic fluid: liquid secreted by the amniotic sac, which supports and protects the fetus

fetus: an unborn mammal, in which all the organs have been formed

IN THIS INVESTIGATION YOU WILL:

model how the amniotic fluid in the uterus protects the growing fetus.

YOU WILL NEED:

- chicken egg × 2   • metre stick or tape measure   • sealable plastic bag × 2
- newspapers.

Safety

- Clear all belongings from the testing area and line with newspapers.
- Be aware of any spillages on the floor.

Getting started

It is not practical to carry out investigations in this unit but, like all scientists, it is important that you are still able to observe parts of the unit in action. Although you will be using chicken eggs, this section will model how the fetus is protected in humans. Discuss with your partner why it is important that scientists (and teachers) use models when trying to explain science.

Method

1   Place an egg into each of the bags.

> **TIP**
>
> Use eggs that are the same size and preferably from the same source.

2   Fill one of the bags to the top with water and seal both bags securely.

3   Prepare the area for testing – this area needs to be clear of personal belongings, books and electrical equipment.

4   Drop the bag that contains the egg and no water from a height of 1 m.

5   Observe and record what happens to the egg.

6   Repeat steps 4 and 5 with the bag that contains the water and the egg.

Recording data

1   Outline what happened to each of the eggs in the investigation.

....

....

....

....

Analysis

2   State which part of the female reproductive system is represented by the water.

....

3   State which part of the reproductive process is represented by the eggs.

....

4   Describe how the answer to Question **2** protects the feature named in Question **3**.

....

....

....

Evaluation

5 Suggest why an egg was dropped without water.

....

....

REFLECTION

How could this investigation be developed further? You may focus on improving reliability, validity or simply personal engagement (for example, you may decide to compare different eggs, or eggs kept in different conditions).

....

....

....

....

EXAM-STYLE QUESTIONS

1 The figure shows the concentration of different hormones during a 28-day cycle of a female human.

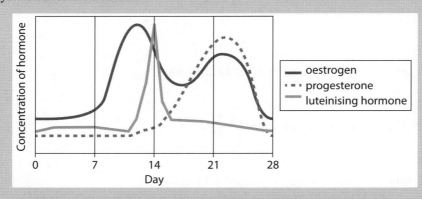

a **State** the name of the gland that produces luteinising hormone.

.... [1]

b State what happens because of the increase in concentration of luteinising hormone on day 14.

.... [1]

c State the names of the hormones in the figure produced in the ovaries.

.... [2]

COMMAND WORD

state: express in clear terms

CONTINUED

d   The concentration of progesterone decreases shortly after day 21. **Explain** why this decrease happens and what happens as a result of the decrease.

....

.... [3]

e   **Suggest** and explain what would happen to the concentration of progesterone after day 21 if the female became pregnant.

....

....

.... [3]

[Total: 10]

2   The figure shows a human fetus during pregnancy.

a   State the name of the structure labelled X.

.... [1]

b   **Describe** the function of X.

.... [2]

c   Suggest why the figure shows a fetus and not an embryo.

....

.... [2]

d   State the name of substances that may be exchanged at the part named Y.

....

....

.... [3]

[Total: 8]

Inheritance

Practical investigation 16.1: Cloning a cauliflower

KEY WORDS

asexual reproduction: a process resulting in the production of genetically identical offspring from one parent

cauliflower floret: one of the smaller flowering stems that make up the head of a cauliflower

clone: make an identical copy of something

explant: cells or tissue that has been transferred from an organism to a nutrient medium

IN THIS INVESTIGATION YOU WILL:

- apply your knowledge of asexual reproduction to clone a cauliflower floret in less than two weeks

- compare the cloned cauliflower to its parent.

YOU WILL NEED:

- small piece / floret of cauliflower • forceps • scalpel • disinfectant solution
- 50 cm³ glass beaker • stopwatch • distilled water (sterile)
- 250 cm³ glass beaker × 2 • Petri dish × 2 • Bunsen burner
- test-tube containing agar growth medium × 2 • aluminium foil • marker pen
- safety spectacles • disposable gloves • aprons/lab coats.

Safety

- Wear gloves when handling the disinfectant and wash hands afterwards.

- Wear protective apron or lab coat.

- Take care using the Bunsen burner and beware of the hot forceps after flaming.

- Take care when using the scalpel.

- Contamination leads to growth of fungi and bacteria. Your teacher will observe the growth of the cauliflower to ensure that harmful pathogens do not grow.

Getting started

You used the aseptic technique in Chapter 10. To remind you how to 'streak' the agar plate, in the space below draw a large circle that is a similar size to a Petri dish. With a pencil, practise the streaking action to show how you would spread the bacteria around the plate. Why do you think it is important to practise your technique?

Method

This is a lengthy method to avoid contamination of the florets and must be followed carefully. Read the safety considerations before starting.

1   Wipe down the work surfaces with disinfectant.

2   Cut off a small piece of cauliflower floret with the scalpel. The piece of cauliflower should be no longer than 5 mm in any direction.

3   Cut the cauliflower into two small pieces. These pieces are known as explants and should be placed into the 50 cm³ glass beaker that contains the disinfectant solution. Leave the explants in the disinfectant for 15 minutes, giving the beaker a gentle swirl every two minutes.

4   Fill the two 250 cm³ beakers with 100 cm³ of the sterile distilled water and cover to avoid contamination.

> **TIP**
>
> Use the Petri dishes or similar apparatus to ensure the top of the beaker is covered.

5   Turn on the Bunsen burner and place the forceps in the Bunsen flame, then leave the forceps to cool.

6   When the 15 minutes has passed, transfer the explants into the first beaker of distilled water, and leave for one minute.

7   During this minute, sterilise the forceps in the Bunsen flame and leave to cool.

8   Transfer the explants into the second beaker of distilled water and leave for one minute.

9   During this minute, sterilise the forceps again and flame the end of the first test-tube that contains the agar growth medium.

10 Place one of the explants into the test-tube with the cool, flamed forceps and cover tightly with aluminium foil. Do this quickly to minimise contamination.

11 Place the second explant into the second flamed test-tube with the cool, flamed forceps and cover tightly with aluminium foil. Do this quickly to minimise contamination.

12 Leave the tubes in a warm, well-lit location and observe after one week and two weeks.

> **TIP**
>
> Check on your clones every few days as you may produce results faster (or slower) than you expect.

Recording data

1   Outline your observations in the following spaces:

   a   After one week:

   ....

   ....

   b   After two weeks:

   ....

   ....

Analysis

2   **a**   If the new pieces of cauliflower floret that have grown were genetically compared to the original explants, suggest how their DNA would compare.

   ....

   b   Explain your answer to part **a**.

   ....

   ....

Evaluation

3   Outline why this method has many steps to avoid contamination of the plants and the equipment used.

   ....

   ....

REFLECTION

How has carrying out this investigation improved your understanding that asexual reproduction produces clones?

....

....

EXAM-STYLE QUESTIONS

1   A man breeds cats for a living. He breeds a cat with black fur with a cat that has brown fur.

   a   The colour of the fur is an example of one of the cats' phenotypes. **Define** phenotype.

   ....

   .... [1]

> **COMMAND WORD**
>
> **define:** give precise meaning

   b   The cat with black fur is homozygous for black fur. Define homozygous.

   ....

   ....

   .... [2]

   c   The cat with the brown fur is homozygous for brown fur. The allele for black fur is dominant and the allele for the brown fur is recessive.

   i   Define allele.

   .... [1]

   ii   Define dominant.

   .... [1]

   iii   Define recessive.

   .... [1]

   d   Use a Punnett square to predict the likelihood of producing offspring with brown fur.

                                                      Answer: .... [4]

   e   **State** the likelihood of producing offspring with black fur.

> **COMMAND WORD**
>
> **state:** express in clear terms

   .... [1]

                                                              [Total: 11]

CONTINUED

2   Marfan syndrome is an autosomal genetic disorder caused by a dominant
    allele (M) that affects the connective tissue. Sufferers of Marfan syndrome
    tend to be tall and thin with long fingers and toes. The FBN1 gene has been
    identified as being the source of genetic mutation in those that suffer from the
    syndrome. The figure shows a pedigree diagram showing the inheritance of
    Marfan syndrome in a family.

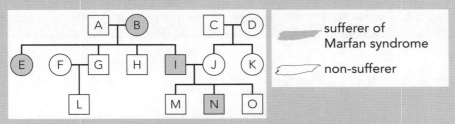

a   Draw the symbol that shows each of the following:

    i   Male non-sufferer   [1]

    ii   Male with Marfan syndrome   [1]

    iii   Female non-sufferer   [1]

    iv   Female with Marfan syndrome   [1]

i   ii   iii   iv

b   i   Using the figure, complete the table to show many people in the
        family pedigree chart fit each description.   [6]

Description	Number of people
Male	9
Female	
Male with Marfan syndrome	
Female with Marfan syndrome	
Homozygous dominant	
Homozygous recessive	
Heterozygous	

    ii   **Explain** why individual B is heterozygous.

....

.... [2]

[Total: 12]

COMMAND WORD

explain: set out
purposes or
reasons / make
the relationships
between things
evident / provide
why and/or how and
support with relevant
evidence

Chapter 17

Variation and natural selection

THE INVESTIGATIONS IN THIS CHAPTER WILL:

- explore how humans show variation
- observe the adaptive features of a leaf that is adapted for survival.

Practical investigation 17.1: Variation in humans

KEY WORDS

characteristics: visible features of an organism

variation: differences between the individuals of the same species

IN THIS INVESTIGATION YOU WILL:

- explore different inherited characteristics within your class
- use gathered data to suggest patterns and similarities.

YOU WILL NEED:

- tape measure/metre stick • graph paper (1 cm²) • pencil.

Getting started

Calculating the area of an irregular object – such as your hand – can be done with a piece of graph paper and a pencil. Practise the technique before doing the investigation.

1   Draw around your outstretched hand onto graph paper (with 1 cm squares). Fill in the gap where your wrist meets the palm, in order the close the drawing up.

2   Count all of the complete squares inside the sketch.

3   Add up all of the parts of squares (such as two half squares would count as one whole square).

4   Add the totals from step 2 and 3 together.

5   Multiply the answer to step 4 by the area of 1 square (1 cm × 1 cm = 1 cm^2).

Method

1   You are going to survey the following features of all of your classmates.

   a   Height / m – use the tape measure/metre stick
   b   Arm span / m – use the tape measure
   c   Hand size / cm^2 – using the graph paper, draw around the hand and calculate the total area

> **TIP**
>
> Use the technique from Getting started to calculate your hand size.

   d   Eye colour

> **TIP**
>
> Make a list of the possible eye colour categories for your class before you begin.

   e   Hair colour

2   Prepare a table in the Recording data section.

3   Complete your table by surveying your classmates.

Recording data

1 Prepare your table in the space provided.

Handling data

2 Look at the data collected in your table.

 a Divide the data gathered for hand size into five suitable categories. For example, 80–100 cm², 101–120 cm², etc. Tally the number of students that fit into each category.

Hand size / cm²	Number of students

 b Draw a histogram to show the results for hand size of the people in your class.

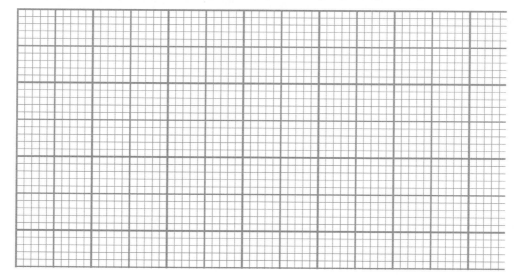

3 Plot a bar chart to show the number of students with each eye colour.

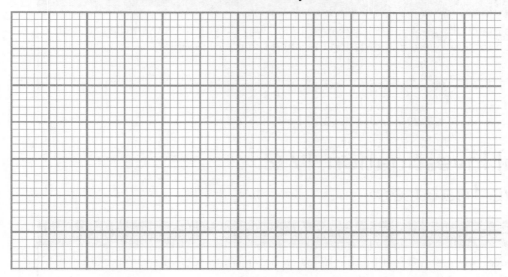

Analysis

4 Describe the pattern of variation for hand size in your class.

....

....

5 State whether the data for hand size is an example of continuous or discontinuous variation.

....

....

6 State any characteristics in this investigation that may be inherited.

....

....

Evaluation

7 Outline how you could improve the reliability of the data that you have collected.

....

....

8 Does your survey reflect the trends across the whole world? Explain your answer.

....

....

REFLECTION

Do your tallies match those of your classmates? If not, why do you think the tallies are not the same, given that you were investigating the same sample of people?

....

....

Practical investigation 17.2: Adaptive features

KEY WORDS

adaptive feature: an inherited feature that helps an organism to survive and reproduce in its environment

IN THIS INVESTIGATION YOU WILL:

observe one of the main adaptive features of a leaf that helps plants to survive in their environment.

YOU WILL NEED:

- leaf from a plant kept in sunlight   • leaf from a plant kept in darkness
- clear nail varnish   • microscope slide   • light microscope
- transparent cellophane tape.

Safety

Wash hands if skin is in contact with nail varnish.

Getting started

It might have been a long time since you used a microscope in Chapter 6. Practise your microscope skills, using pre-prepared slides of common cells. Can you use the highest magnification to finely focus the image? You will need to use the focusing wheel to do so.

Method

1   Label each of the leaves for identification later. Add a thick layer of the clear nail varnish to the underside of one of the leaves.

2   Allow the nail varnish to dry completely. This can take several minutes for some varnishes.

> **TIP**
>
> Use a hairdryer, hand dryer or a radiator to speed up the drying of your leaf.

3   Once the varnish is hard and dry, place a piece of the cellophane tape over the varnished area and gently peel it back. This will lift the varnish from the leaf, and the tape now contains an imprint of the underside of the leaf.

> **TIP**
>
> Avoid the central vein (midrib) when applying the nail varnish to the underside of the leaf. This will make it easier to peel off the varnish and produce a flat specimen.

4   Place your varnish sample onto the microscope slide and trim away any excess tape.

5   Observe under the light microscope at a magnification of ×400. Locate an area with several stomata in clear view.

6   Make a labelled drawing of what you see in the Recording data section.

7   Repeat steps 1–6 for the second leaf.

Recording data

1   Make a labelled drawing of what you can see in the field of view for each of the two leaves.

leaf in sunlight

leaf in darkness

Handling data

2   Count the number of open stomata in each of the samples.

   a   Leaf in sunlight:

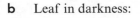

   b   Leaf in darkness:

....

Analysis

3 Explain the difference between the numbers of open stomata that you observed.

....

....

....

Evaluation

4 Suggest why it is important to use leaves from the same species of plant in this investigation.

....

....

5 Suggest how the comparison of open stomata in darkness and in light could be made more reliable in this investigation.

....

....

EXAM-STYLE QUESTIONS

1 A teacher is carrying out a survey to gather data about the mass of the students who attend his classes. He surveys 69 students and records their mass in categories in the following table.

Mass / kg	Number of boys	Number of girls
30–40	2	2
41–50	9	7
51–60	14	12
61–70	6	7
71–80	5	2
81+	2	1

a **State** the type of variation that the teacher has measured.

.... [1]

COMMAND WORD

state: express in clear terms

CONTINUED

b Draw a suitable graph/chart to show the data collected by the teacher.

[4]

c **Describe** the pattern of data collected by the teacher.

....

.... [2]

d **Suggest** one reason why the data for the mass of the students can be considered reliable.

.... [1]

[Total: 8]

COMMAND WORDS

describe: state the points of a topic / give characteristics and main features

suggest: apply knowledge and understanding to situations where there are a range of valid responses in order to make proposals / put forward considerations

Chapter 18

Organisms and their environment

THE INVESTIGATIONS IN THIS CHAPTER WILL:

- allow you to observe population sizes of organisms and assess the biodiversity of the area

- help you to construct a compost using household materials.

Practical investigation 18.1: Using a quadrat

KEY WORDS

habitat: the place where an organism lives

population: a group of organisms of one species, living in the same area at the same time

quadrat: portable frame used to mark out an area for counting organisms

IN THIS INVESTIGATION YOU WILL:

observe population sizes for organisms in your local area.

YOU WILL NEED:

- quadrat • smartphone or digital camera.

Safety

- Do not handle any organisms with your hands.
- Do not remove any organisms from their natural habitat.
- Do not throw the quadrat in the direction of other students.

Getting started

You will be using a quadrat for the investigation. What is the best method of selecting where to place / throw the quadrat? How could you eliminate bias from your selections?

Method

1 Observe the area that you are going to survey. You will need to select how many times you will place your quadrat and where you will place it.

2 Place the quadrat in your chosen areas.

3 For each quadrat, count the number of each species (either plant, animal or both) that is present in that area.

4 Collate your data with others in your class.

> **TIP**
>
> If you do not know the name of a species, take a photograph of it, make a note of it in your table in the Recording data section and use this to research the species name later.

5 Note the environmental conditions of each quadrat – level of light, shade, access to water, predators or animals present.

6 Repeat the quadrat sample as directed by your teacher. It is better to collect as much data from as many different areas as possible.

Recording data

1 Prepare a table in the following space to record the population sizes for each quadrat sample taken.

Handling data

2 Draw a bar chart to show the relative population sizes for the species counted in the area surveyed.

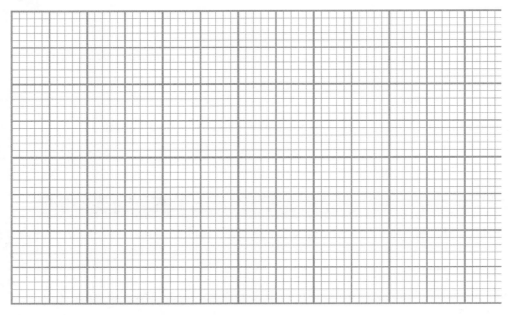

Analysis

3 Describe the data that you have collected from this investigation.

....

....

....

4 Discuss how the population size of the organisms that you surveyed varies between different areas.

....

....

....

5 Suggest why some areas had larger populations of the same species than others.

....

....

....

Evaluation

6 Explain why more than one quadrat sample was taken.

....

....

7 Explain why a quadrat should be placed in *random* locations during an investigation.

....

....

8 Suggest why you did not count every single organism for the area covered in the investigation.

....

....

REFLECTION

Think about the number of times you placed your quadrat. How could you improve the reliability of your results if you were to do the investigation again?

....

....

Practical investigation 18.2: Making compost

IN THIS INVESTIGATION YOU WILL:

construct your own compost column and observe which materials decompose.

YOU WILL NEED:

- 2-litre plastic bottle • 1 kg soil • kitchen waste • non-biodegradable waste
- organic waste • scissors • mounted needle • Bunsen burner • insulation tape
- water • pipette • aluminium foil • elastic band.

Safety

- Take care when using the scissors.
- Cover any jagged edges of plastic with insulation tape to avoid cuts.
- Wash hands after handling waste or soil.
- Do not add dairy or meat products as they will smell.

Getting started

You are required to use the Bunsen burner for the investigation. What are the steps that you should take to light your Bunsen burner safely? Before starting the investigation, practise turning on your Bunsen burner safely with the yellow flame. The air hole should be fully closed.

Method

1   Use the scissors to cut off the top of the plastic bottle at the point where the label begins (remove the label).

2   Fill the bottom third of the bottle with soil.

3   Add a loose layer of organic waste and a loose layer of soil.

4   Pipette enough water to provide some moisture to the layer.

5   Add a loose layer of kitchen waste and a loose layer of soil.

6   Pipette enough water to provide some moisture to the layer.

7   Add a loose layer of non-biodegradable waste and a loose layer of soil.

8   Pipette enough water to provide some moisture to the layer.

9   Turn on the Bunsen burner and heat the end of the mounted needle.

10   When the needle is red-hot, use the needle to pierce several small holes on the side of the bottle. The holes must be small enough to avoid the soil spilling out.

11   Cover the top of the bottle with the foil and secure with the elastic band. Pierce a few holes in the foil. Place the bottles in an area where they will receive sunlight and not get too hot, or too cold.

12   Observe the bottles after 4, 8 and 12 weeks.

> **TIP**
>
> Shaking the bottle gently every few days will ensure that enough air can get into the bottle.

Recording data

1   Record your observations of what happens inside the compost bottle.

Date compost made:

....

4-week date and observation:

....

....

8-week date and observation:

....

....

12-week date and observation:

....

....

Analysis

2   Describe the difference between the rates of decomposition for the three different types of waste in your compost column.

....

....

3   It is possible to test for nitrates with nitrate strips. State the layer of your compost that would most likely test positive for nitrates or nitrites. Explain the reasons for your answer.

....

....

....

4   State the name of the chemical reaction that breaks down plant and animal protein to ammonium ions.

....

5   Suggest how the addition of worms to your compost would affect the rate of decomposition for your waste products.

....

....

EXAM-STYLE QUESTIONS

1   The figure shows the changes for a population of bacteria.

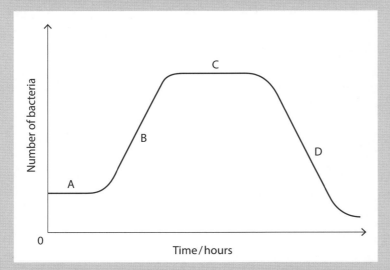

a   **State** the name of the phase in part A of the curve.

.... [1]

b   State the name of the phase in part B of the curve.

.... [1]

c   State the name of the phase in part C of the curve.

.... [1]

d   State the name of the phase in part D of the curve.

.... [1]

e   **Explain** why the rate of growth increases in part B of the curve.

....

.... [2]

f   **Suggest** why the population decreases in part D of the curve.

....

....

.... [3]

[Total: 9]

COMMAND WORDS

state: express in clear terms

explain: set out purposes or reasons / make the relationships between things evident / provide why and/or how and support with relevant evidence

suggest: apply knowledge and understanding to situations where there are a range of valid responses in order to make proposals / put forward considerations

CONTINUED

2   A student investigates the number of caterpillars found in different gardens in her street and records her data in the table.

Garden	Number of caterpillars found in each garden
A	2
B	4
C	8
D	1
E	0
F	6
G	7

a   **Calculate** the average number of caterpillars found in the gardens, using information from the table.

[3]

COMMAND WORD

calculate: work out from given facts, figures or information

b   The student counts the total number of gardens in the street to be 32. Use this information to estimate the total number of caterpillars found in gardens in her street.

[2]

c   Suggest why the total number of caterpillars found in the gardens of the street might not be accurate.

....

.... [1]

[Total: 6]

> Chapter 19

Human influences on ecosystems

THE INVESTIGATIONS IN THIS CHAPTER WILL:

- show how humans have affected the environment
- observe the effects of the combustion of fossil fuels.

Practical investigation 19.1: Effect of acid on the germination of cress seeds

KEY WORDS

germination: when a seed develops into a plant

saturate: to soak something completely

IN THIS INVESTIGATION YOU WILL:

investigate the effect of acid on the germination of cress seeds.

YOU WILL NEED:

- cress seeds • dilute acid of different concentrations • pipettes • paper towels
- Petri dish × 4 • distilled water • safety spectacles • disposable gloves.

Safety

Wash hands if in contact with irritant acids.

Getting started

This investigation requires the use of more than one concentration of acid. Your results require that the acids are not too similar in concentration. What safety precautions will you need to take to ensure safe use of the acids? What will you do in the event that an acid is spilled onto you or the work surface?

Method

1   Select three acids at different concentrations for this investigation. Record the concentrations in the table in the Recording data section.

2   Prepare four Petri dishes with a paper towel in the bottom of each dish.

3   Place eight cress seeds into each of the Petri dishes.

> **TIP**
>
> Place the seeds equal distances apart to allow room for growth.

4   Pour enough of the acid solution to saturate each of the paper towels, and saturate the fourth paper towel with distilled water.

5   Observe what happens in seven days and record your observations.

Recording data

1   Record the different concentrations of your acid solutions and your observations in the table.

Cress seeds 'watered' with:	Observation after seven days
distilled water	
acid .... mol dm^{-3}	
acid .... mol dm^{-3}	
acid .... mol dm^{-3}	

Analysis

2 Describe the effect the different acid solutions had on the germination rate of the cress seeds.

....

....

3 Explain the effect the different acid solutions had on the germination rate of the cress seeds.

....

....

4 Suggest how the investigation shows the effect that human activity can have on the environment.

....

....

....

Evaluation

5 Suggest how the investigation could be improved to produce data that compares the growth rate of the cress seedlings.

....

....

....

6 Suggest how your method could be improved to be more reliable.

....

....

....

Practical investigation 19.2:
Fossil fuel combustion

KEY WORDS

acid rain: rain that is more acidic due to the presence of gases produced by combustion of fossil fuels

universal indicator: solution that changes colour depending on the pH of the solution being tested

IN THIS INVESTIGATION YOU WILL:

- observe what happens when coal is heated

- link your observation to human impact on ecosystems.

YOU WILL NEED:

- small lumps of coal • Bunsen burner • boss clamp and stand • cotton wool
- heat mat • double delivery tube system (see Figure 19.1) • universal indicator
- conical flask • vacuum pump or fume cupboard • safety spectacles.

Safety

- Carry out the investigation in a fume cupboard (your teacher will demonstrate this) or by using a vacuum pump to collect the gases formed by the combustion of the coal.

- Take care when using the hot Bunsen burner and do not handle the equipment until it has cooled.

Getting started

You will be using a vacuum pump or fume cupboard for the investigation. If you have not used a vacuum pump before, you will need to become familiar with the equipment first. Practise operating the pump and be confident that you are using it correctly before starting the investigation.

Method

1 Set up the equipment as shown in Figure 19.1.

2 Turn on the Bunsen burner and begin to heat the coal.

3 Observe what happens to the cotton wool and the universal indicator.

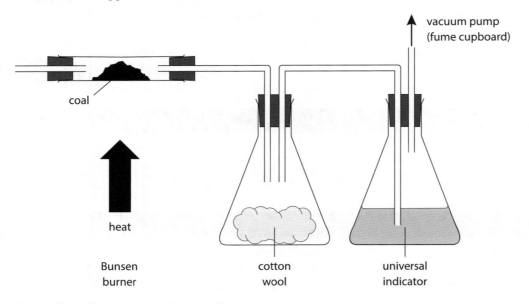

Figure 19.1: Equipment needed.

Recording data

1 In the space below, draw and label a diagram to show what happened to the cotton wool and the universal indicator in the investigation.

Handling data

2   Describe the effect that burning coal had on:

a   The cotton wool

....

b   The universal indicator

....

Analysis

3   Suggest how the change in colour of the universal indicator supports your understanding of how acid rain is formed.

....

....

4   Predict and explain what would happen if the investigation was repeated using limewater in place of the universal indicator.

....

....

Evaluation

5   Suggest how you could investigate the effect of burning different quantities of coal on the acidity of the gases produced.

....

....

....

....

....

REFLECTION

Compare your results with those of your classmates. Do you agree with the observations of your classmates? Why do you think scientists like to find a way to measure what they can see?

....

....

....

EXAM-STYLE QUESTIONS

1 A student is investigating the effect of burning fossil fuels. The student burns a known fossil fuel and predicts that there will be acidic gases produced. If the student is correct, which of the following should she expect to see?

A Universal indicator turns blue

B Universal indicator turns orange / red

C Red cabbage indicator turns blue

D pH paper turns white .... [1]

2 A student investigates the quality of soil in different locations and records his results into the table. He measures the pH using two different methods.

Garden area	Colour of universal indicator	pH measured by pH probe
A	Green	6.9
B	Light green / yellow	5.4
C	Yellow	4.7

a **State** which garden area would be most suitable for growing garden plants that prefer neutral conditions.

.... [1]

b **Explain** your answer for part **a**.

....

.... [1]

c Explain why the pH probe is more suitable for investigating the pH of the soil.

....

.... [2]

d **Suggest** what might have caused garden area C to have a lower pH.

....

.... [3]

e The student decides to use the soil samples in the laboratory to test the effect of the different pH on plant growth. State two variables that he must keep constant in the investigation.

....

.... [2]

[Total: 9]

COMMAND WORDS

state: express in clear terms

explain: set out purposes or reasons / make the relationships between things evident / provide why and/or how and support with relevant evidence

suggest: apply knowledge and understanding to situations where there are a range of valid responses in order to make proposals / put forward considerations

Chapter 20

Biotechnology and genetic modification

THE INVESTIGATIONS IN THIS CHAPTER WILL:

- look at how bacteria are useful in biotechnology
- allow you to observe the action of pectinase in commercial juice production
- allow you to observe the difference between biological and non-biological washing powders.

Practical investigation 20.1: Effect of pectinase on apple pulp

KEY WORD

pectinase: an enzyme that is used to digest pectin, increasing the quantity of juice that can be extracted from fruit, and clarifying the juice

IN THIS INVESTIGATION YOU WILL:

observe the effect of the enzyme pectinase on apple pulp.

YOU WILL NEED:

- 100 g of apple • 250 cm³ glass beaker × 2 • 100 cm³ measuring cylinder × 2
- glass stirring rod × 2 • stopwatch • balance • pectinase
- water-bath or incubator, 40 °C • knife • water • chopping board
- plastic wrap • funnel × 2 • filter paper × 2.

Safety

- Take care when using the scalpel or knife.
- Handle pectinase with care. Wash hands after use or if contact is made with the pectinase.
- Immediately clean up any spillages.

Getting started

Chopping the apple into small, equal pieces requires patience and skill. You and your lab partner should practise doing so with some plasticine, ensuring that you keep your fingers out of the way for safety.

Method

1   Chop the apple into small, equal pieces. These should be no larger than 5 mm³.

> **TIP**
>
> Cut the strips of apple lengthways first. It is easier to chop the strips into equal-sided cubes.

2   Divide the 100 g of apple into two separate beakers.

3   Add 2 cm³ of pectinase to one of the beakers and stir with the glass rod.

4   Add 2 cm³ of water to the second beaker of apple and stir with the glass rod.

5   Cover the beakers with plastic wrap and incubate at 40 °C for 20 minutes.

6   Line the funnels with the filter paper.

7   Place the funnel over the measuring cylinder and add the pulp from each beaker.

8   Record the volume of juice obtained from each sample of apple pulp every five minutes until the juice no longer filters through the paper.

Recording data

1   Record your data in the table.

Apple	Volume of juice produced / cm³							
	0 minutes	5 minutes	10 minutes	15 minutes	20 minutes	25 minutes	30 minutes	35 minutes
with pectinase								
in water								

Handling data

2   Draw a line graph to show the amount of apple juice produced over time when pectinase is added.

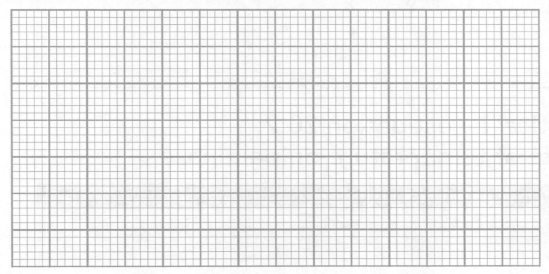

Analysis

3   Describe the effect of pectinase on the amount of juice produced from apple pulp.

....

....

4   Explain why the effect of pectinase is important in the commercial production of apple juice from pulp.

....

....

....

Evaluation

5   Suggest why the investigation was carried out using water.

....

....

6   Were all of the apple samples from the same apple? If not, were the apples all of the same type of apple? How might this affect your results?

....

....

REFLECTION

How has the investigation supported your understanding of the action of pectinase on apple pulp and its use in biotechnology?

....

....

Practical investigation 20.2: Effect of temperature on pectinase

IN THIS INVESTIGATION YOU WILL:

plan your own investigation to see at which temperature pectinase will work most effectively.

YOU WILL NEED:

- 100 g of apple   • 250 cm^3 glass beakers   • 100 cm^3 measuring cylinders
- glass stirring rods   • stopwatch   • balance   • pectinase
- water-bath or incubator   • knife   • chopping board   • plastic wrap
- funnels   • filter paper   • safety spectacles.

Safety

Wash your hands after handling pectinase.

1   State two other safety precautions that you must take.

....

....

Getting started

You will be observing the action of an enzyme called pectinase. Pectinase is an enzyme that is present in apple pulp. Use your knowledge of enzymes to suggest the ideal temperature to observe the action of pectinase in your investigation.

Method

2   Your task is to plan a method that will allow you to compare the effect of pectinase at three different temperatures. Plan your method below.

   • Identify your independent variable (what you will change) and state how you will change this variable.

   • Identify your dependent variable (what you will measure), how you will measure it and how long you will observe it for.

   • Identify all other possible variables or conditions and state how you will keep them the same.

   These three steps will support you in writing a good method.

   ....

   ....

   ....

   ....

   ....

   ....

   ....

   ....

   ....

   ....

3   State the three different temperatures at which you will test the effect of pectinase on apple pulp.

   a   .... °C   b   .... °C   c   .... °C

Recording data

4   Prepare a table to record the total amount of juice produced from apple pulp at the three different temperatures selected.

Analysis

5   State the temperature at which pectinase worked best on the apple pulp.

....

6   Suggest how you know that your answer for Question 5 is the temperature at which pectinase worked best.

....

....

7   Use your knowledge of enzymes to suggest why the pectinase worked best at this temperature.

....

....

....

Evaluation

8   Outline how the reliability and validity of the investigation could be improved.

....

....

....

....

Practical investigation 20.3: Biological washing powders

KEY WORDS

biological washing powder: washing powder that contains enzymes

non-biological washing powder: washing powder that does not contain enzymes

IN THIS INVESTIGATION YOU WILL:

investigate the effect of different washing powders on removing egg stains from a piece of material.

YOU WILL NEED:

- piece of white material × 2 • egg • paper towels • tablespoon • plastic tray
- 250 cm³ glass beaker × 2 • 100 cm³ glass beaker • stirring rod • kettle
- biological washing powder • non-biological washing powder • stopwatch.

Safety

- Wash hands after handling the washing powders and egg.
- Clean the work surfaces with disinfectant.

Getting started

Have you ever considered which type of washing powder / detergent works best on removing stains? Make predictions about the type of washing powder that will be best at removing stains and dirt.

Method

1   Break the egg into the $100\,cm^3$ glass beaker.

2   Stir the egg to break the yolk and mix the contents.

3   Over the plastic tray, spoon some of the egg mixture onto the white material. Use your hands to rub the egg into the material. Use the paper towel to absorb any excess egg.

4   Leave the material to dry.

> **TIP**
>
> Drying the material will be much faster in a warm place, such as in direct sunlight or by a heat source.

5   In the meantime, prepare the beakers and label accordingly. Add $200\,cm^3$ of warm water from the kettle (as close to 40–50 °C as possible) to each of the $250\,cm^3$ glass beakers.

6   Add two tablespoons of the biological washing powder to one of the beakers, and two tablespoons of the non-biological washing powder to the second beaker.

7   Add the two pieces of stained material to the beakers at the same time. Check that they are both at the same temperature, and begin the stopwatch.

8   Leave the material in the water for 15 minutes before removing. Then dry near a heat source, such as a radiator or in direct sunlight.

9   Observe the difference in stains and record your observations in the Recording data section.

Recording data

1   Draw and label the difference between the two pieces of material in the boxes below.

biological washing powder   non-biological washing powder

Analysis

2   Describe the difference in the stains after being soaked in the washing powder solutions.

....

....

3   Suggest the reasons for your results.

....

....

4   Eggs contain protein. Suggest the name of an enzyme that would be suitable for breaking down the egg stains.

....

Evaluation

5   Outline how you could investigate the effect of the biological washing powder at different temperatures.

....

....

....

....

....

EXAM-STYLE QUESTIONS

1   a   A control was used when comparing the effect of pectinase on breaking down apple pulp. What was the reason for using a control?

   A   To improve reliability.

   B   To improve accuracy of the results.

   C   To be able to compare the effect with and without pectinase.

   D   To release the pectinase from the walls.   .... [1]

CONTINUED

b Pectinase, protease and lipase are useful enzymes in industry and at home.

Describe and **explain** how the enzymes are used in the home or in industry.

....

....

....

....

....

....

....

....

....

....

.... [6]

c Describe a method to test the effect of pH on the activity of pectinase.

....

....

....

....

.... [5]

d **Suggest** two variables that the student would need to control in the investigation.

....

.... [2]

[Total: 14]

COMMAND WORDS

describe: state the points of a topic / give characteristics and main features

explain: set out purposes or reasons / make the relationships between things evident / provide why and/or how and support with relevant evidence

suggest: apply knowledge and understanding to situations where there are a range of valid responses in order to make proposals / put forward considerations

> Glossary

Command Words

Below are the Cambridge International definitions for command words which may be used in exams. The information in this section is taken from the Cambridge IGCSE Biology syllabus (0610/0970) for examination from 2023. You should always refer to the appropriate syllabus document for the year of your examination to confirm the details and for more information. The syllabus document is available on the Cambridge International website www.cambridgeinternational.org.

calculate: work out from given facts, figures or information

compare: identify/comment on similarities and/or differences

define: give precise meaning

describe: state the points of a topic / give characteristics and main features

determine: establish an answer using the information available

evaluate: judge or calculate the quality, importance, amount, or value of something

explain: set out purposes or reasons / make the relationships between things evident / provide why and/or how and support with relevant evidence

give: produce an answer from a given source or recall/memory

identify: name/select/recognise

outline: set out main points

predict: suggest what may happen based on available information

sketch: make a simple freehand drawing showing the key features, taking care over proportions

state: express in clear terms

suggest: apply knowledge and understanding to situations where there are a range of valid responses in order to make proposals / put forward considerations

Key Words

acid rain: rain that is more acidic due to the presence of gases produced by combustion of fossil fuels

adaptive feature: an inherited feature that helps an organism to survive and reproduce in its environment

alkaline pyrogallol: caustic substance that removes oxygen

amniotic fluid: liquid secreted by the amniotic sac, which supports and protects the fetus

amylase: an enzyme that catalyses the breakdown of starch to maltose

anhydrous copper sulfate: a copper salt that turns blue in the presence of water

antibacterial mouthwash: solution used to destroy bacteria in the mouth

aorta: the largest artery in the body, which receives oxygenated blood from the left ventricle and delivers it to the body organs

aseptic technique: technique used to sterilise equipment and destroy all pathogens

asexual reproduction: a process resulting in the production of genetically identical offspring from one parent

Benedict's solution: a blue liquid that turns orange-red when heated with reducing sugar

biological drawing: used to represent the visible features of an organism, in the correct size, shape and proportion

biological washing powder: washing powder that contains enzymes

biuret reagent: a blue solution that turns purple when mixed with amino acids or proteins

breathing rate: the number of breaths taken per minute

carpel: the female part of a flower

catalase: an enzyme that catalyses the breakdown of hydrogen peroxide to water and oxygen

cauliflower floret: one of the smaller flowering stems that make up the head of a cauliflower

characteristics: visible features of an organism

clone: make an identical copy of something

concentration gradient: an imaginary 'slope' from a high concentration to a low concentration

cortex: the tissue making up the outer layer in a kidney

DCPIP: a purple liquid that becomes colourless when mixed with vitamin C

dependent variable: the variable that you measure, as you collect your results

dichotomous key: a way of identifying an organism, by working through pairs of statements that lead you to its name

diffusion: the net movement of particles from a region of their higher concentration to a region of their lower concentration (i.e. down a concentration gradient), as a result of their random movement

dissect: dissecting an animal (or plant) to observe internal parts

DNA: a molecule that contains genetic information, in the form of genes, that controls the proteins that are made in the cell

enamel: the very strong material that covers the surface of a tooth

enzyme activity: the rate at which an enzyme works

enzymes: proteins that are involved in all metabolic reactions, where they function as biological catalysts

evaporation: when a liquid changes to a gas

explant: cells or tissue that has been transferred from an organism to a nutrient medium

fats: lipids that are solid at room temperature

feature: parts of an organism that you can see; also known as characteristics, e.g. the fur of a mammal

fetus: an unborn mammal, in which all the organs have been formed

germination: when a seed develops into a plant

habitat: the place where an organism lives

heart rate: the number of beats per minute of the heart

independent variable: the variable that you change in an experiment

inoculating loop: a tool used by biologists to transfer a sample to a Petri dish

inverting: turning an object upside down

iodine solution: a solution of iodine in potassium iodide; it is orange-brown, and turns blue-black when mixed with starch

joules: unit for measuring energy

light microscope: a type of microscope that uses light and a lens to magnify a specimen

limiting factor: a factor that is in short supply, which stops an activity (such as photosynthesis) happening at a faster rate

longitudinal cut: a cut made along the long axis of a structure

magnification: how many times larger an image is than the actual object. If an object is drawn smaller than its actual size, then the magnification is less than 1.

medulla: the tissue making up the inner layers in a kidney

non-biological washing powder: washing powder that does not contain enzymes

osmosis: the diffusion of water molecules through a partially permeable membrane

oxygen debt: extra oxygen that is needed after anaerobic respiration has taken place, in order to break down the lactic acid produced

pectinase: an enzyme that is used to digest pectin, increasing the quantity of juice that can be extracted from fruit, and clarifying the juice

Petri dish: shallow dish used to culture microorganisms

photosynthesis: the process by which plants synthesise carbohydrates from raw materials using energy from light

population: a group of organisms of one species, living in the same area at the same time

potometer: used to measure the rate of transpiration in a plant

protein: a substance whose molecules are made of many amino acids linked together; each different protein has a different sequence of amino acids

pulmonary veins: the veins that carry oxygenated blood from the lungs to the left atrium of the heart

pulse: throbbing of the arteries in the wrist or neck due to blood flowing through them

quadrat: portable frame used to mark out an area for counting organisms

reaction time: time taken to respond to a stimulus

reducing sugars: sugars such as glucose, which turn Benedict's solution orange-red when heated together

response: behaviour that results from a stimulus

saturate: to soak something completely

sensitivity: the ability to detect and respond to changes in the internal or external environment

sepals: leaf-like structures that form a ring outside the petals of a flower

specific heat capacity of water: energy required to heat 1 g of water by 1 °C

specimen: a prepared slide that contains something viewed under a microscope

staining solution: used to make cells more visible on a microscope slide, such as iodine or methylene blue

stamens: the male parts of a flower

starch: a carbohydrate that is used as an energy store in plant cells

sterile: free from microorganisms and pathogens

stimuli: changes in the environment that can be detected by organisms

stomata (singular: **stoma**): openings in the surface of a leaf, most commonly in the lower surface; they are surrounded by pairs of guard cells, which control whether the stomata are open or closed

thermoregulation: the process that allows the temperature of the body to be maintained

transpiration: the loss of water vapour from leaves

universal indicator: solution that changes colour depending on the pH of the solution being tested

variation: differences between the individuals of the same species

xylem: a plant tissue made up of dead, empty cells joined end to end; it transports water and mineral ions and helps to support the plant